Roger White

Roger White

The Pedestrian

INVENTORY PRESS

The Transparency of the Everyday	Helen Molesworth	6
Plates		12
Picture Time	Ross Simonini	98
Acknowledgments		102

The Transparency of the Everyday

Helen Molesworth

Containers

Why is Roger White's watercolor of a Brita water pitcher so compelling? There's the pleasure of recognition, of possession (I have one at home), of identification (we are the same). There's the optical illusion of water, air, and the light that makes these things visible. There's empty and full—here doing double duty as positive and negative space. There's the subdued monochrome, the leaching of color, the play of white on white, silver on gray. There's medium specificity—watercolor for the water pitcher. There's the history of art, all those vanitas and still life paintings, genre scenes filled with glasses of water reflecting and refracting light. The spirit of prestidigitation, the love of the trick. There's the pleasure of its banality. Not that the Brita pitcher is banal, the Brita is wildly symbolic, laden with a surfeit of meaning connoting everything from our unending reliance on petroleum by-products to the corporate contamination of our drinking water, which in turn opens the floodgates onto our current climate catastrophe and some garden variety necropolitics; so, no, the Brita is not banal as such. What is on display in the watercolor is the banality of the contemporary itself. What feels banal is that the "contemporary" or the "now" can only ever be represented by something relatively inconsequential, something tangential, something you putatively don't notice, something you could live without, something that won't be saved. Note that the three oil paintings, *Lid*, *Container (II)*, and *Container (III)*, are all images of plastic clamshells. *Container (III)* offers us the type designed for strawberries, doubtless picked by migrant workers to be purchased and consumed by coastal elites year-round. Such delicate berries were once imaged with tender affection, easily bruised, appearing only in early summer, their appearance in a seventeenth- or eighteenth-century still life would have signified the embarrassment of riches alongside the fleeting pleasures of life, the surety of death, the inexorable passing of time. One of the oddest, most discomforting things about White's play with the tour de force tropes of transparency that have governed still life painting is this shift from the transitory impermanence of life to the potential permanence, now measured in half-lives, of our plastic world. (When I asked the internet how long it took a plastic container to decompose, an AI bot offered that a plastic bottle takes 450 years to decompose and "even then" its molecules are still in the soil, water, and air.) White's watercolors of plastic containers elevate something already deeply germane to the genre, namely that there is "something miraculous and sad about the glass on the table. Water disciplined into a vertical cylinder. The depressing spectacle of our triumph over the elements."[1]

Calendars

What is the future? That unknowable yawn of time that opens out before us every time we close our eyes to sleep, every time we open our eyes into wakefulness. The future is never dinner. Dinner is the everyday, the now; dinner is tonight. Dinner is the future we understand. The future is the realm in which we let our fantasies run wild—utopian or dystopic, merely differences in affect and style. The future is the thing we pretend we can't map and don't know. And yet we know exactly when the tides will be high and low, when the sun will rise and set, when the moon will wax and wane. We know exactly which days will bear which numbers in the Gregorian calendar, which itself dates to 1582 and can be projected into eternity. Roger White makes paintings of the days, months, and years to come. He paints the nexus of knowable and unknowable time each time he paints a calendar. A space of almost pure projection. The canvas as window, looking out into the future, and mirror, the canvas as a surface that reflects the viewer's projections. A few years ago, I noticed Heinrich Wöfflin's (the art historian who gave the discipline two of its most persistent organizational forms—the slide projector and the logic of "compare and contrast") life dates: 1865–1945. They stopped me cold, not out of love for the discipline (of which I am suffused), but for what they foretold. I was born in 1966. I could easily die in 2045. I saw in myself an echo of Wöfflin. I understood my subjectivity anew. I was born in the last century, and I carry with me many of its anachronisms: affection for the popular culture of my grandmother's generation, knowledge of the politics of my parents' generation, and the social mores of my childhood. White's images of generic calendars do the same. In the era of the smartphone, the paper calendar already feels like a vestige of our analog paper-based past. White is not immune to the convention of placing an image above the grid of time. While the days have already been mapped out, images of the future recede into a state of permanent imagination. White has topped his calendars with technicolor abstractions redolent of Gerhard Richter's endgame of painting strategies, although I have often thought Richter's blurs were images of what happens to the color of the sunset now that it is in the process of being permanently altered by the man-made effects of greenhouse gases (a painterly wet dream of the hole in the ozone layer being a foil for negative space). I want this sentence to offer a pithy interpretation. I want to comply with the expectation that I can connect the dots. I want to write something just shy of grandiose about Richter and the end of the modernist project, but I find myself too overwhelmed by the admixture of failed irony and shy saccharine melancholy to pull off any aesthetic pronouncements. Instead, I wonder how different life would be if we had the luxury of knowing our death date. And I wonder, in the face of these calendars of the future, what happens to the status of the future as an outer limit of our imagination when the future is in a state of ambiguity due to climate change. If we can no longer count on the persistence of the past in the space of the present (this is largely how I see the function of our enlightenment institutions such as the museum, the university, and the library), and we have grown tentative about the planet's ability to sustain us moving forward, then does the everyday fall prey to the logic of the catastrophe? There is no romance about the everyday in the realm of catastrophe. The space of catastrophe offers us the everyday as the essentials of life—water, food, shelter. The logic of catastrophe makes mincemeat of monuments and iconic images. White's calendars of the future offer us the twinned diagram of time already accounted for below and its unimaginability as a blur above.

Memory

The effect of the family snapshot is to suture its participants into a shared experience that they can then bank as a common memory. Mostly they end up as fodder: the boredom and mystery of other people's family snapshots (see *Instax*). Our collective fantasy that in a "snap" there is a "shot" that carries with it a germ of the truth. Truth here meaning the ability of a bunch of people to agree upon the terms—the blue of the sky at *Carmel Beach, New Year's Day*, the view through the French door to the pool in *Corral de Tierra*, the ensuite bathroom at the *Paseo Hermoso*.

Like the watercolor of the Brita, these delicately rendered, nearly perfectly chromatic explorations, these pictures of everyday life in White's hands might just be working to stave off the disappointments of everyday life. They subtly refuse the grave ennui of "is that all there is" with a prosaic sensitivity to postwar suburban space and its inhabitants (see *San Benancio Canyon*). White's paintings recall Dave Hickey's admonishment that "very few works of art venture into the haunted realm—the elusiveness and mystery—of everyday life."[2] The tug of a Roger White image is precisely in this place. One cannot live in the space of catastrophe and disappointment. One assembles one's reality to defend against the realities of catastrophe and disappointment. One makes pictures and writes books in order to convey one's version of things, to offer one's sense of things as factual, to confirm one's experience as a form of evidence. This is one of the ways we understand the realism of representational imagery. This is part of where its magic and disappointment emanate from. The world is either represented too closely to its appearance or not closely enough. Too specific to be universal, too universal to break through to the ego. More Dave Hickey: "The world always means more. Its opacity is more interesting."[3]

Still life and snapshots and calendars all work to secure our shared sense of reality. Each document offers a version of objectivity, a desire to show things as they are, to imagine that the categories of the "objective" and "reality" share so much as to be commensurate with one another. And yet, the gentle psychoanalytic theorist D. W. Winnicott reminds us that when we become "so firmly anchored in objectively perceived reality" that we can become "ill in the opposite direction of being out of touch with the subjective world and with the creative approach to fact."[4] If the opacity of the everyday is always more beguiling than our representations of it, then might the entanglement between an objective presentation and "creative approach to fact" be the place of last resort for capturing the ineffable impossible quandary of the everyday? It seems to me that is what's at stake in the watercolor *The Artist's Mother*. An aerial view, we look down on a large tree, a house, a hedgerow. Blue skies and midday shadows complete the picture's atmosphere of an endless summer. The mother in question is barely visible. Indeed, sometimes I'm not sure she's even in the picture. Is that small smudge of pink pigment a woman hanging wash on a line? Not that you can see the line, or the crisp sheeting in the wind. Rather there are shadows and smudges and a white shape that can't decide if it's geometric or biomorphic. Here the creative handling of the facts sutures us into the picture, offering the security of the vista, an omnipotent view in which the world unfurls before us. The title makes a promise of intimacy, of revelation, of origins and sentiments. The image subtly demurs. As the aqueous pigment grabs hold of the paper's pulp it softens the hard edge of the photographic nature of our memories. It anticipates the blur of our snapshots and memories. It acknowledges the way an image like this, plucked from the flow of daily time, resists calendar time. The picture is of an event that happened in the past that anticipates the quotidian future of attenuated memory, possessing the same half-life as an ineffable and unremarkable plastic container.

1 Hernan Diaz, *Trust* (Riverhead, 2022), 393.

2 Dave Hickey, "In the Dancehall of the Dead," in *Feint of Heart: Art Writings: 1982–2002* (David Zwirner Books, 2024), 147.

3 Ibid.

4 D. W. Winnicott, *Playing and Reality* (Routledge, 1989 [1971]), 89.

Interstate
2023
Oil on linen
38 × 28 inches
96.5 × 71.1 cm

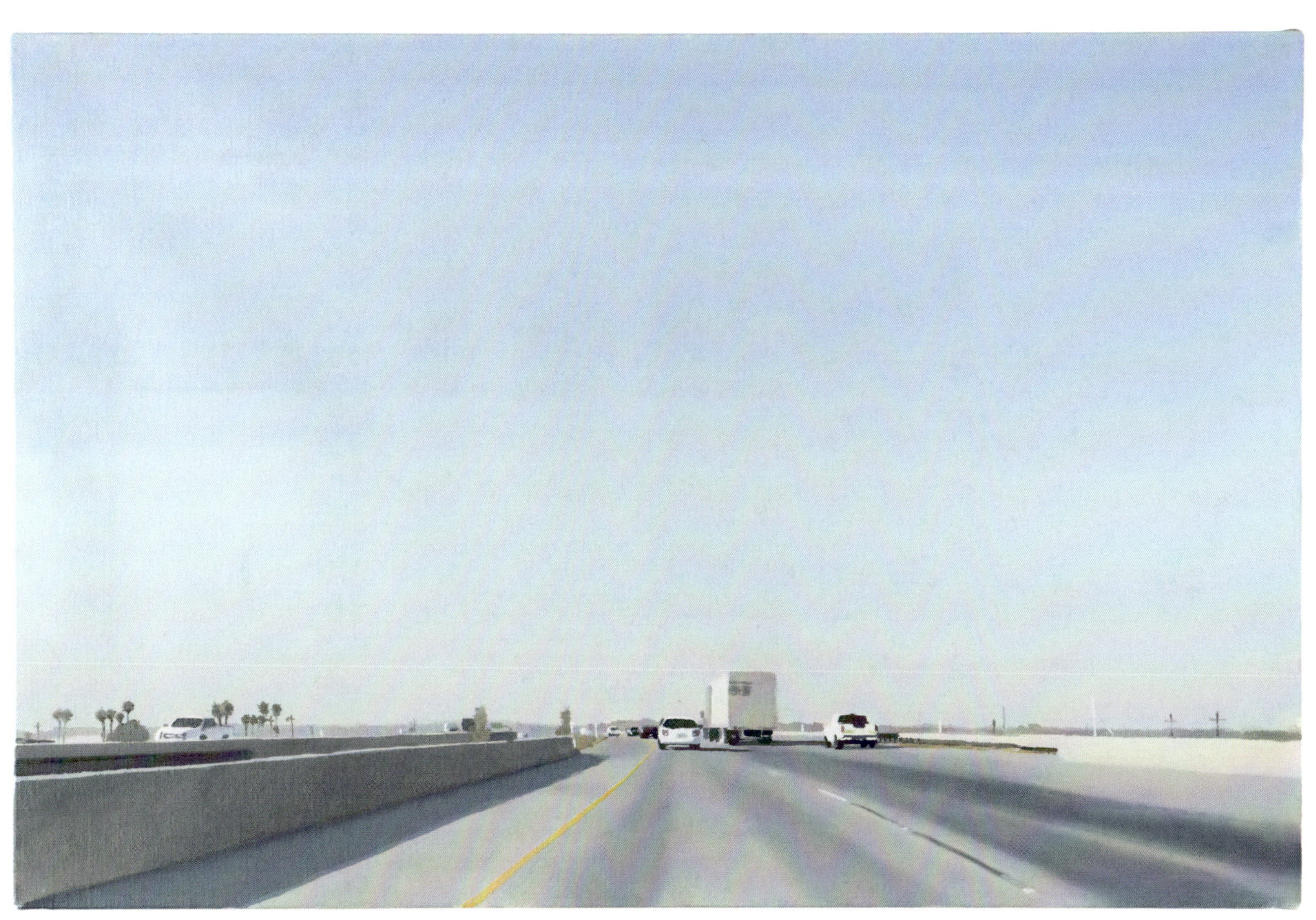

Carmel Beach, New Year's Day
2023–24
Oil on linen
38 × 32 inches
96.5 × 81.3 cm

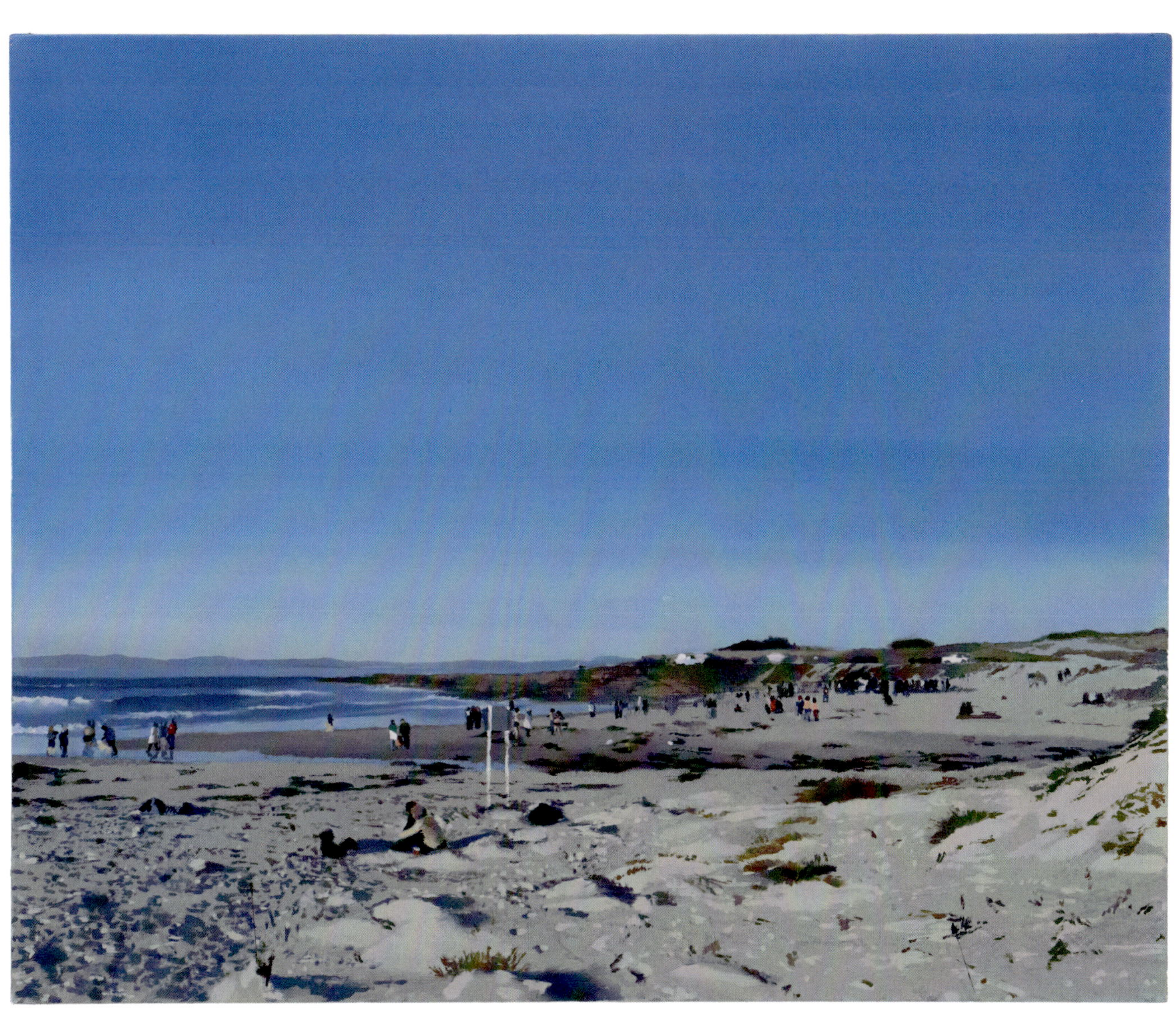

Lid
2023
Oil on linen
12 × 10 inches
30.5 × 25.4 cm

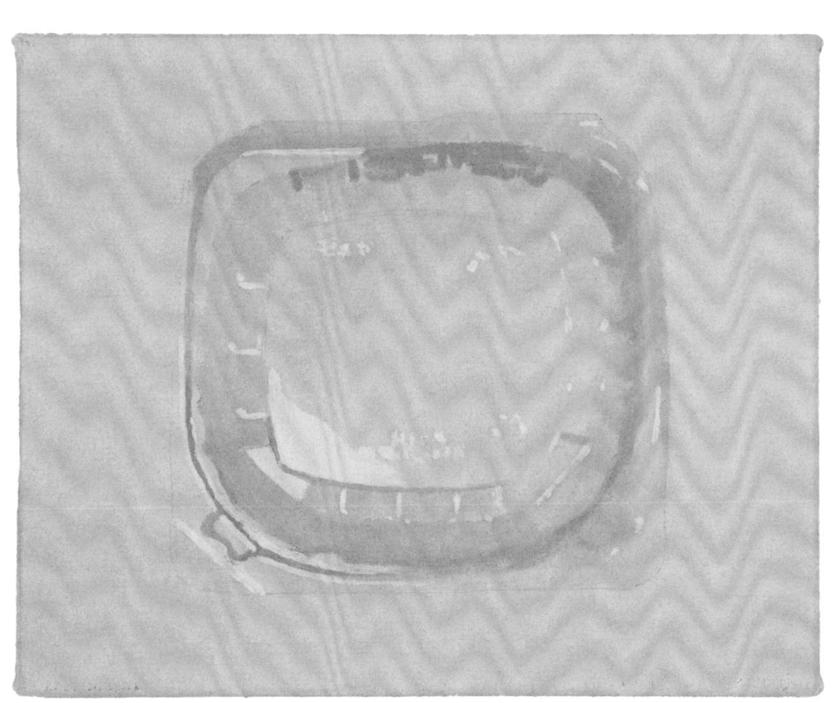

Long Beach
2023–24
Oil on linen
60 × 44 inches
152.4 × 111.8 cm

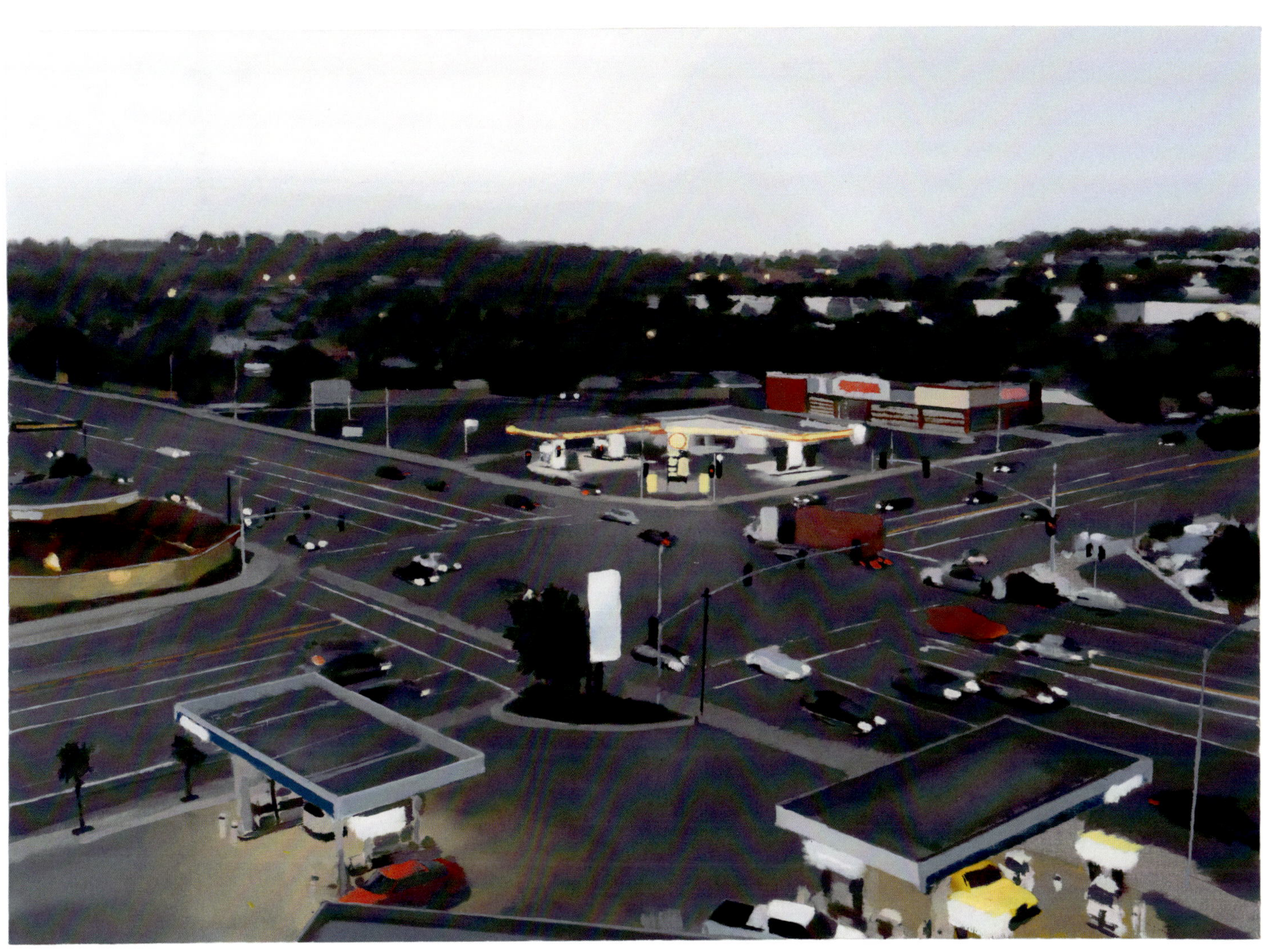

Driscoll's
2023–24
Oil on linen
56 × 54 inches
142.2 × 137.2 cm

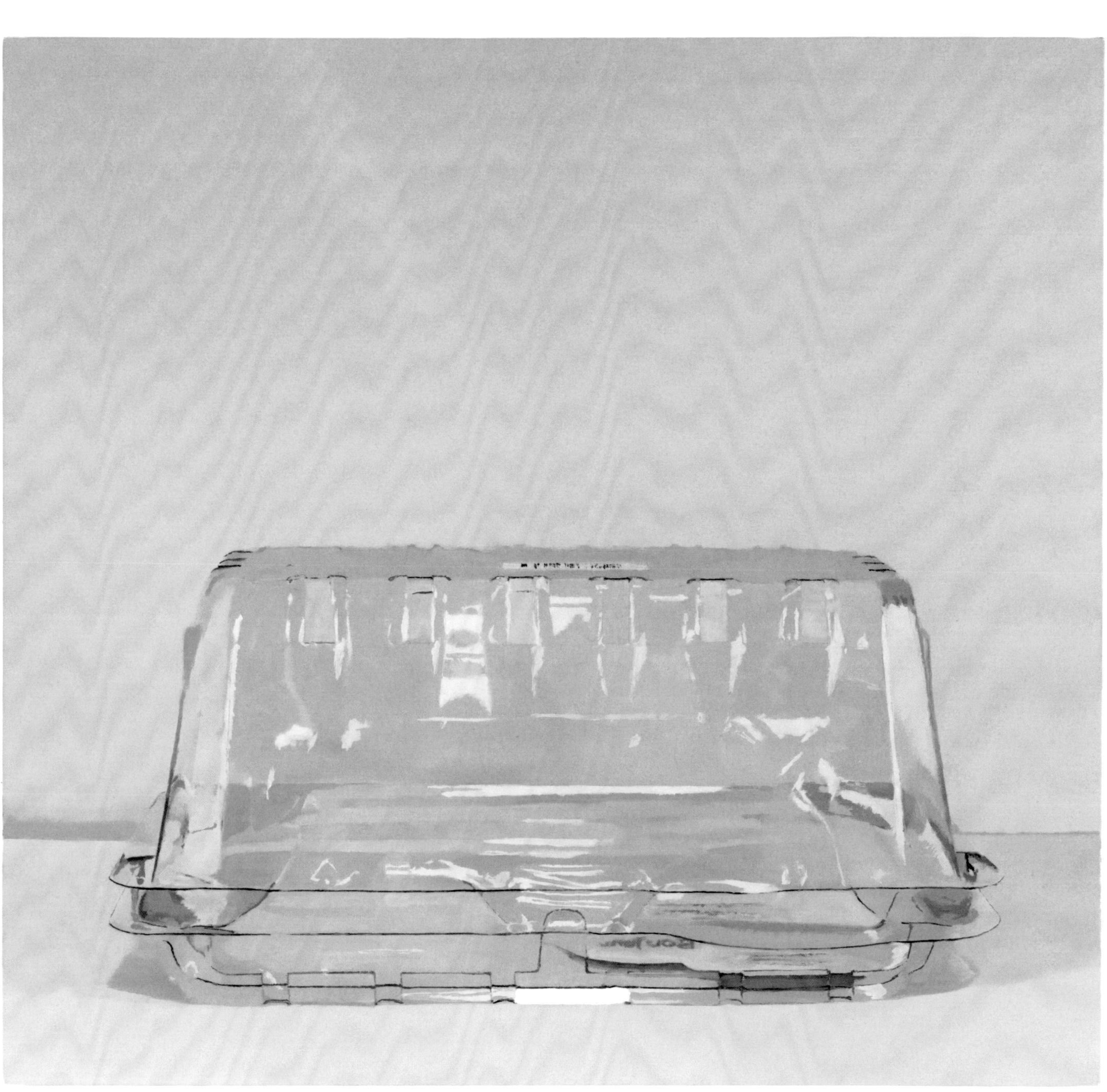

Ryan Ranch
2024
Oil on linen
54 × 37 inches
137.2 × 94 cm

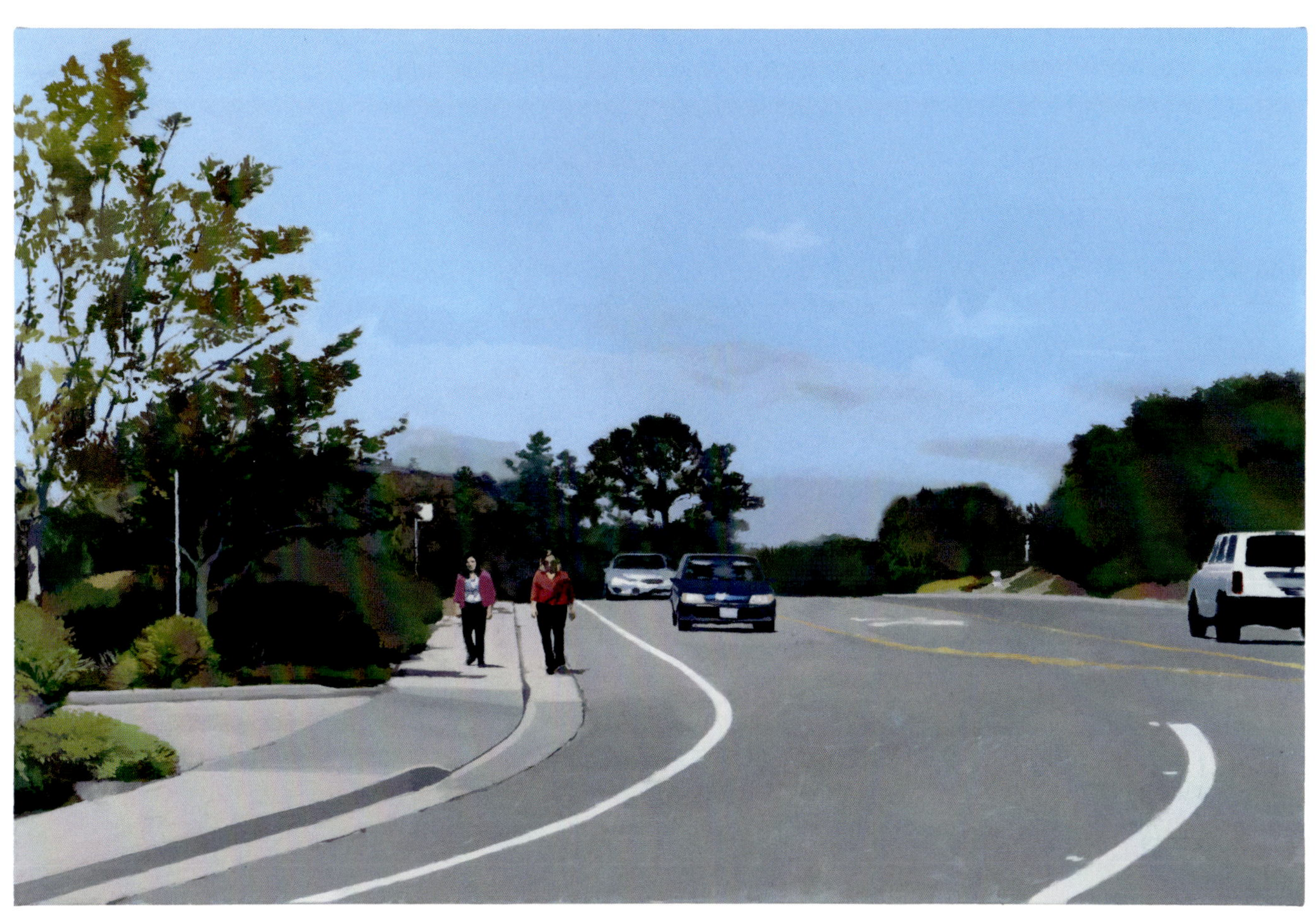

Mission San Diego diorama at Knott's Berry Farm, from a photograph by M. H. Habata
2024
Oil on linen
18 × 18 inches
45.7 × 45.7 cm

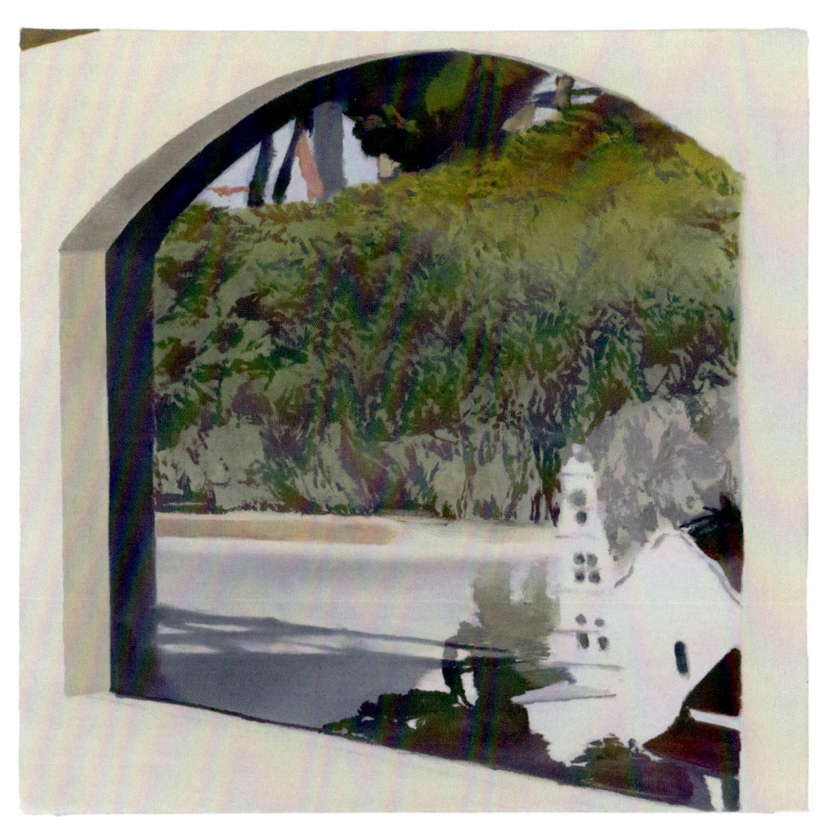

San Benancio Canyon
2023–24
Oil on linen
66 × 50 inches
167.6 × 127 cm

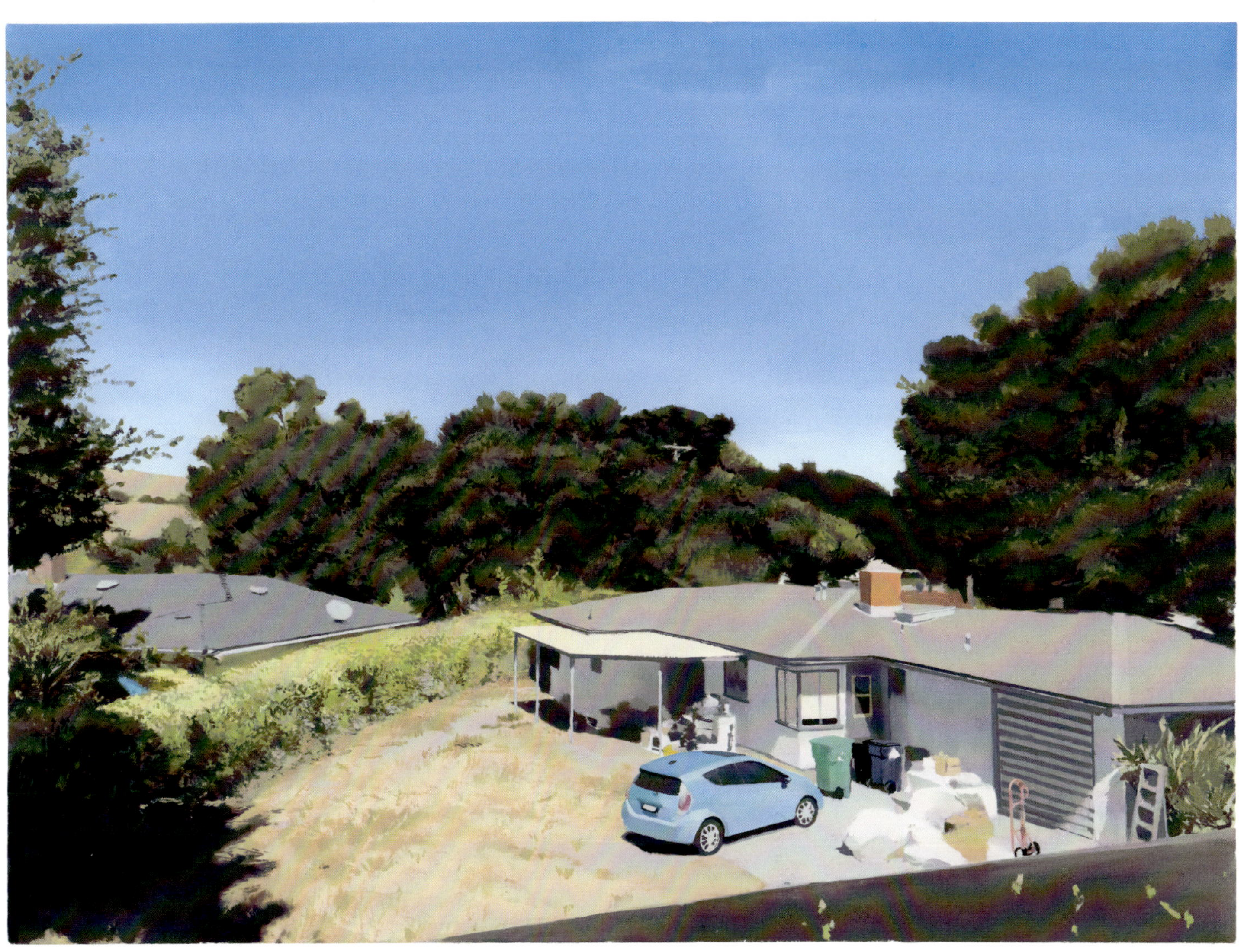

Corral de Tierra
2023–24
Oil on linen
32 × 42 inches
81.3 × 106.7 cm

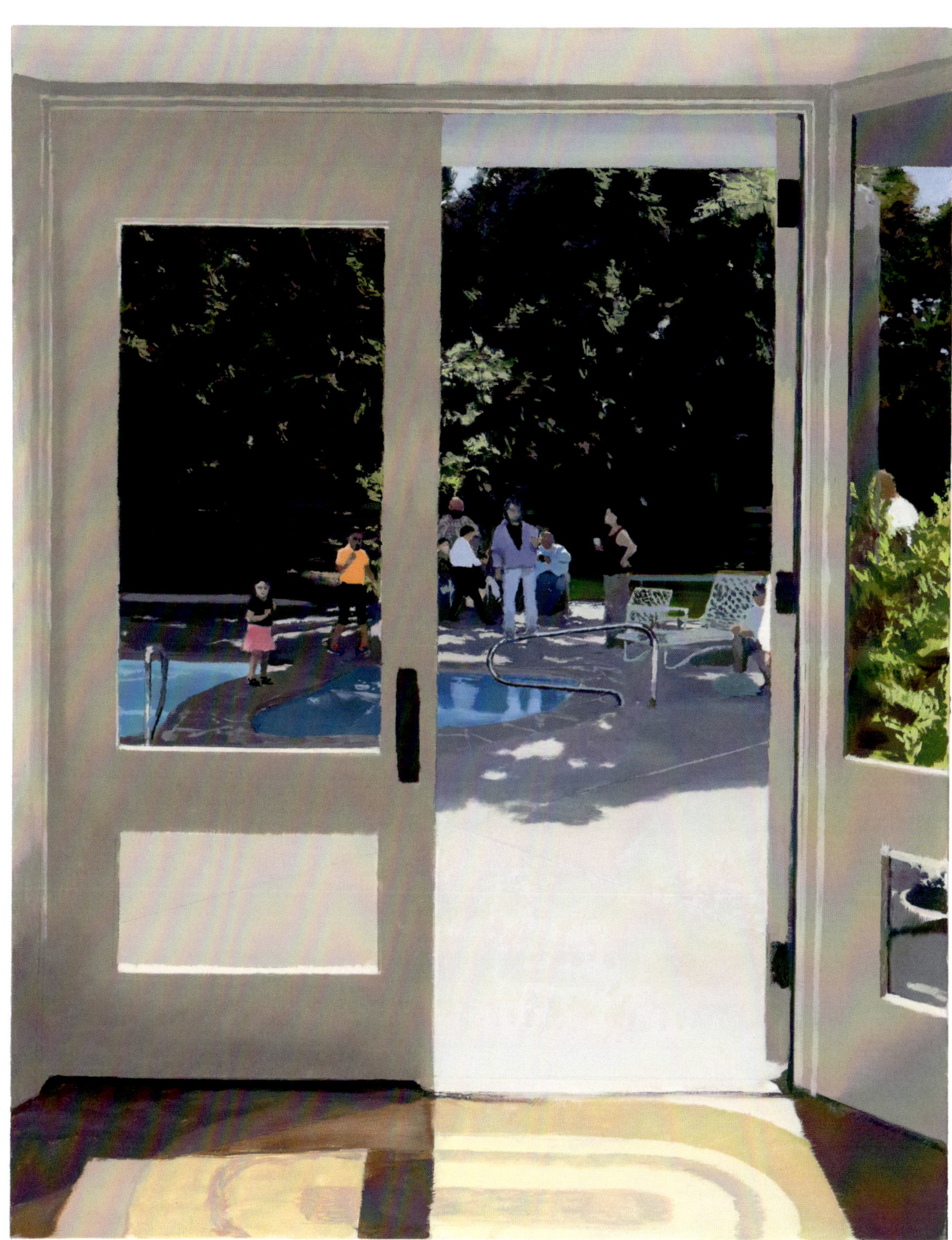

Instax
2024
Oil on linen
31 × 40 inches
78.7 × 101.6 cm

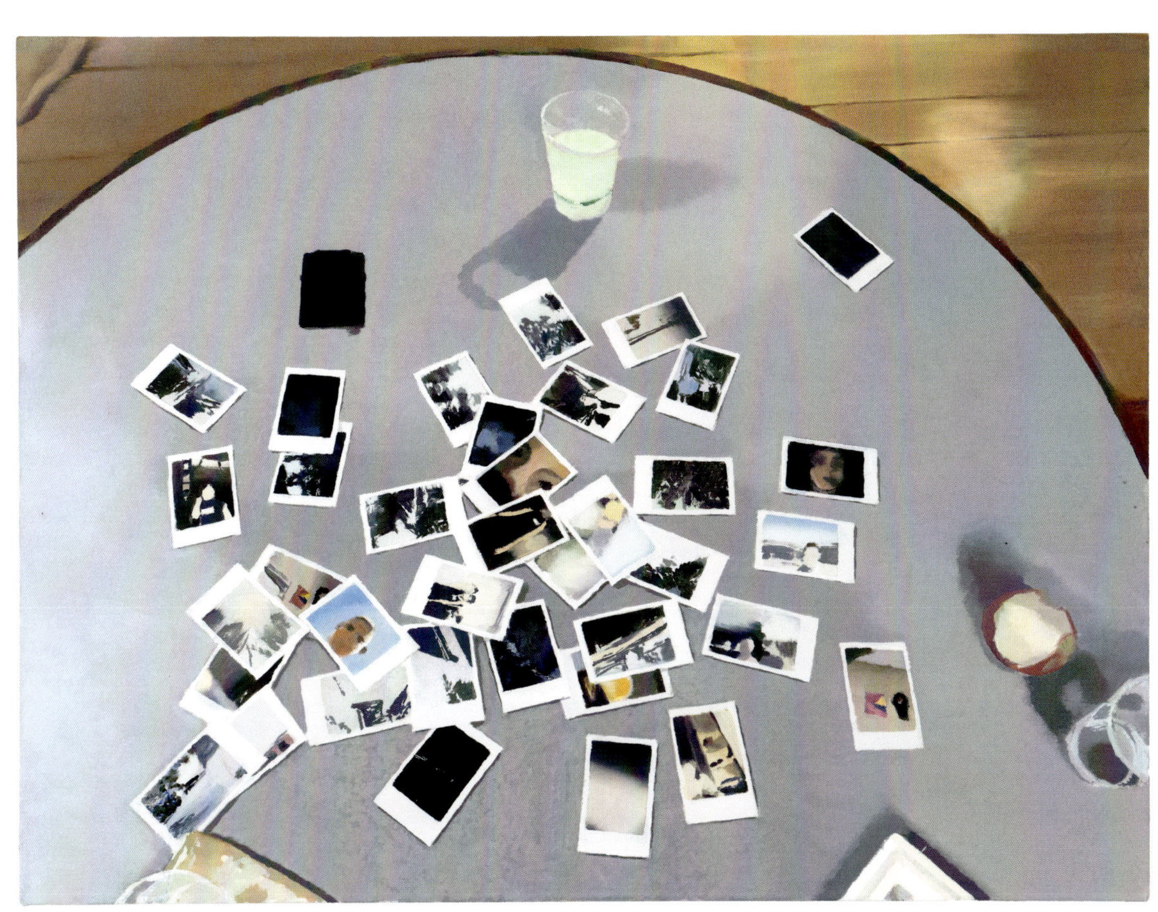

Paseo Hermoso
2023–24
Oil on linen
14 × 18 inches
35.6 × 45.7 cm

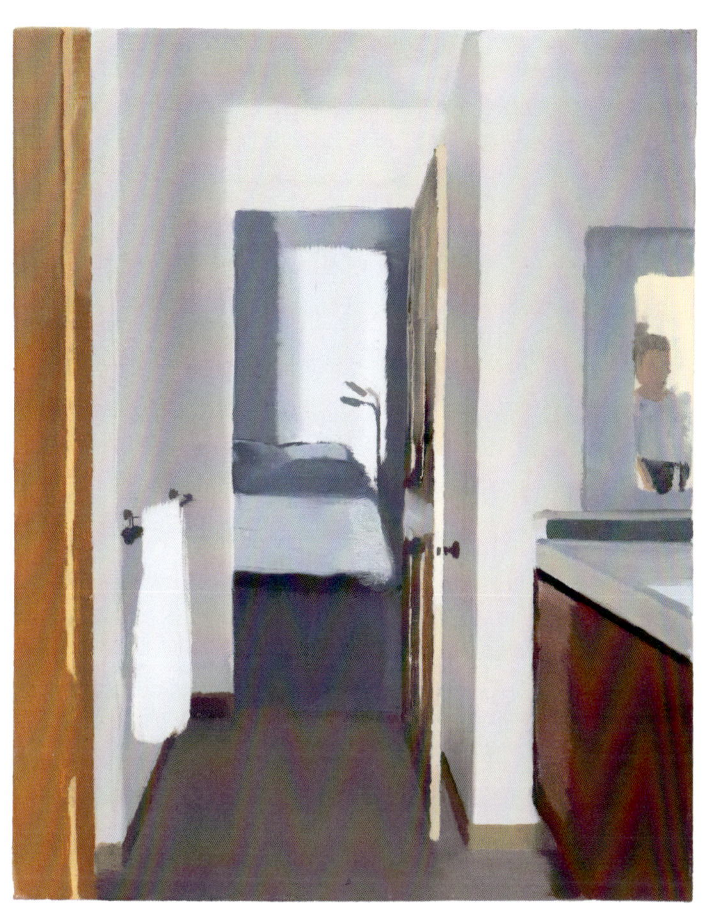

The Bowl (I)
2024
Oil on linen
14 × 18 inches
35.6 × 45.7 cm

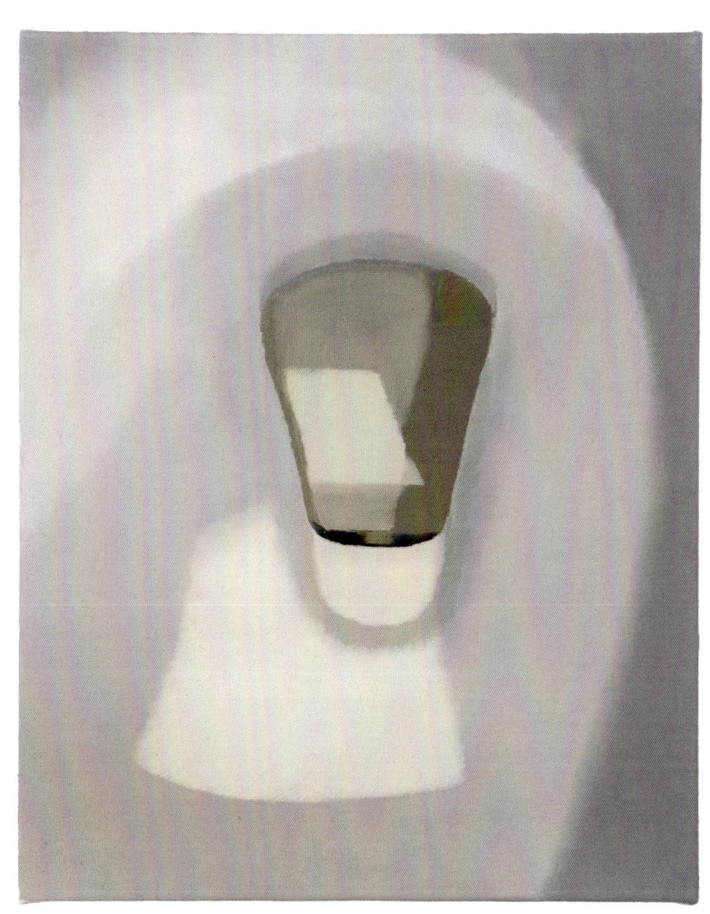

Blank Calendar
2023–24
Oil and pencil on linen
12 panels,
each 14 × 22 inches
35.6 × 55.9 cm

JANUARY

S	M	T	W	Tr	F	Sa

FEBRUARY

S	M	T	W	Tr	F	Sa

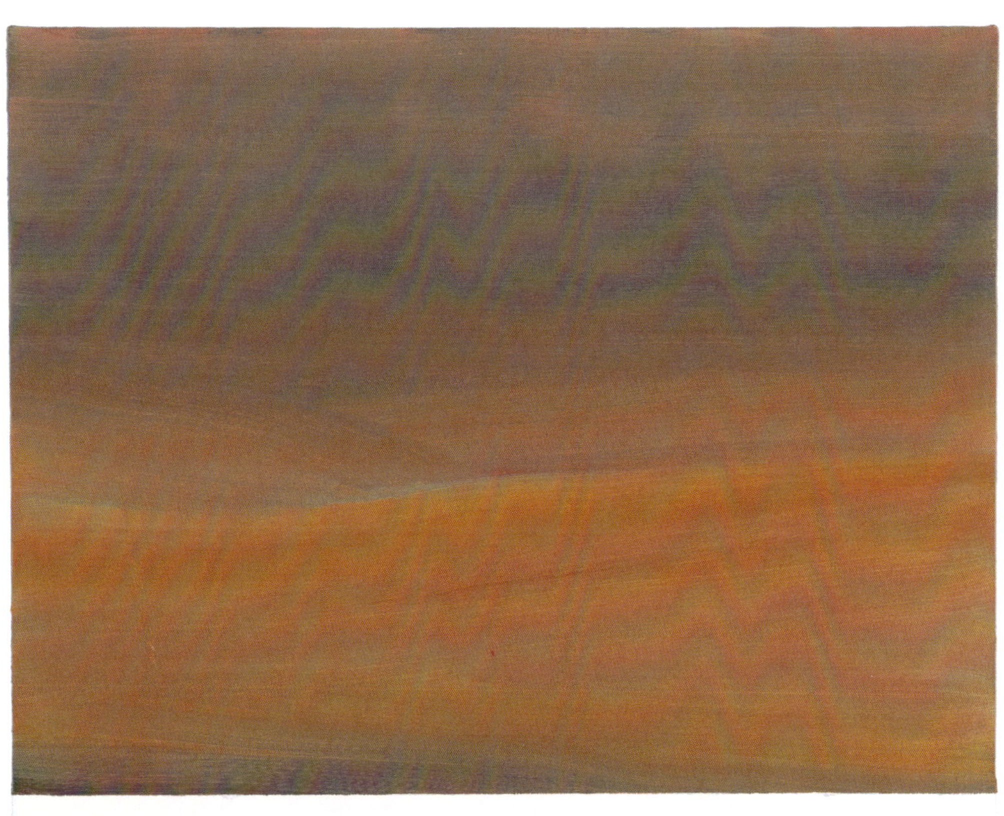

MARCH

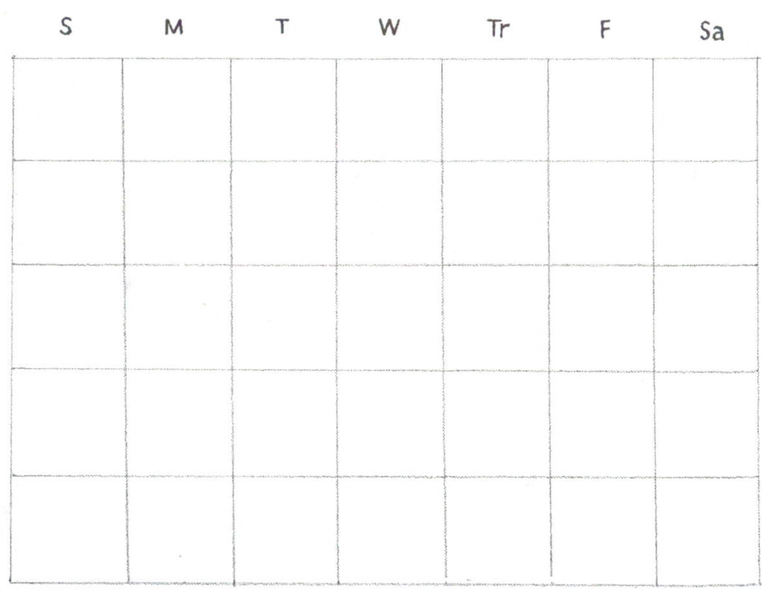

APRIL

S	M	T	W	Tr	F	Sa

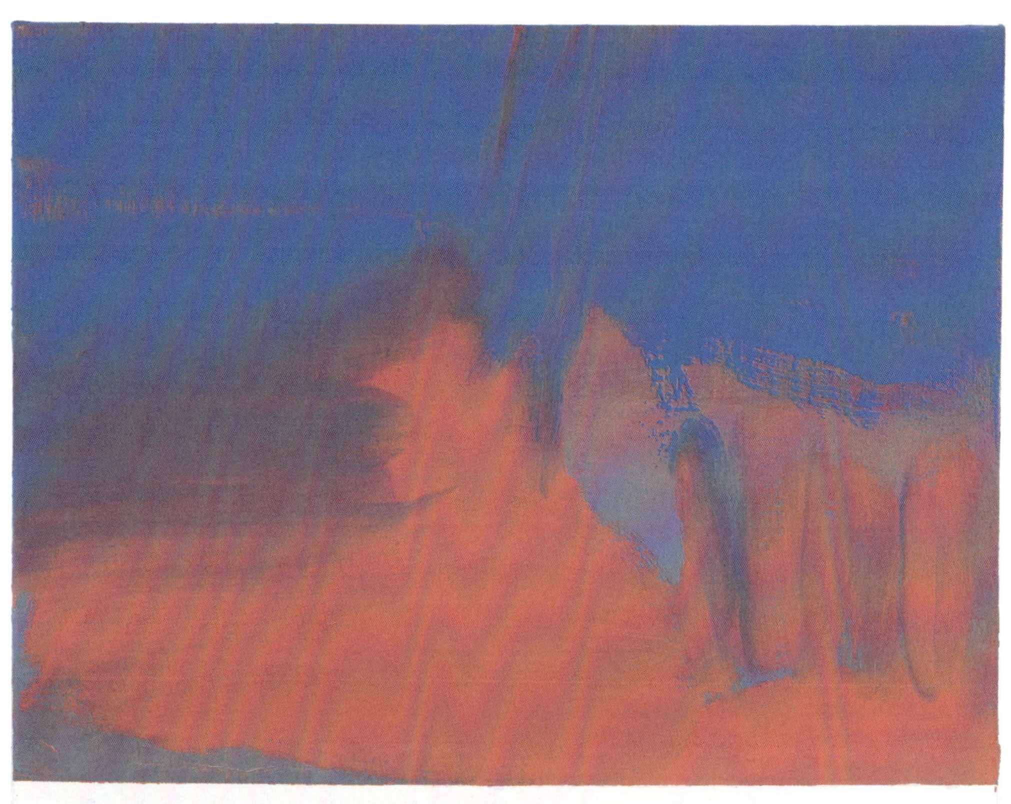

MAY

S	M	T	W	Tr	F	Sa

JUNE

S	M	T	W	Tr	F	Sa

JULY

S	M	T	W	Tr	F	Sa

AUGUST

S	M	T	W	Tr	F	Sa

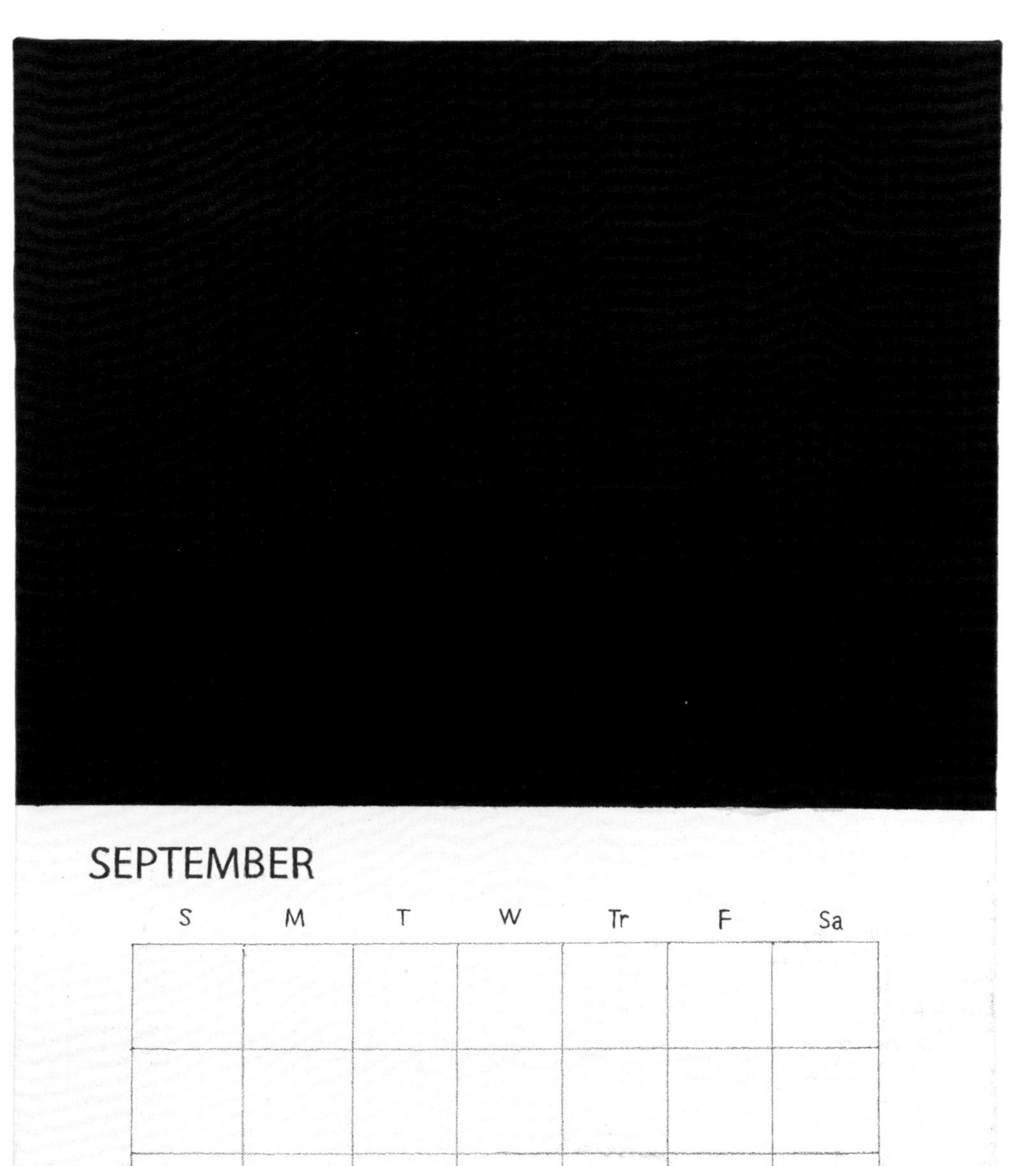
SEPTEMBER
S M T W Tr F Sa

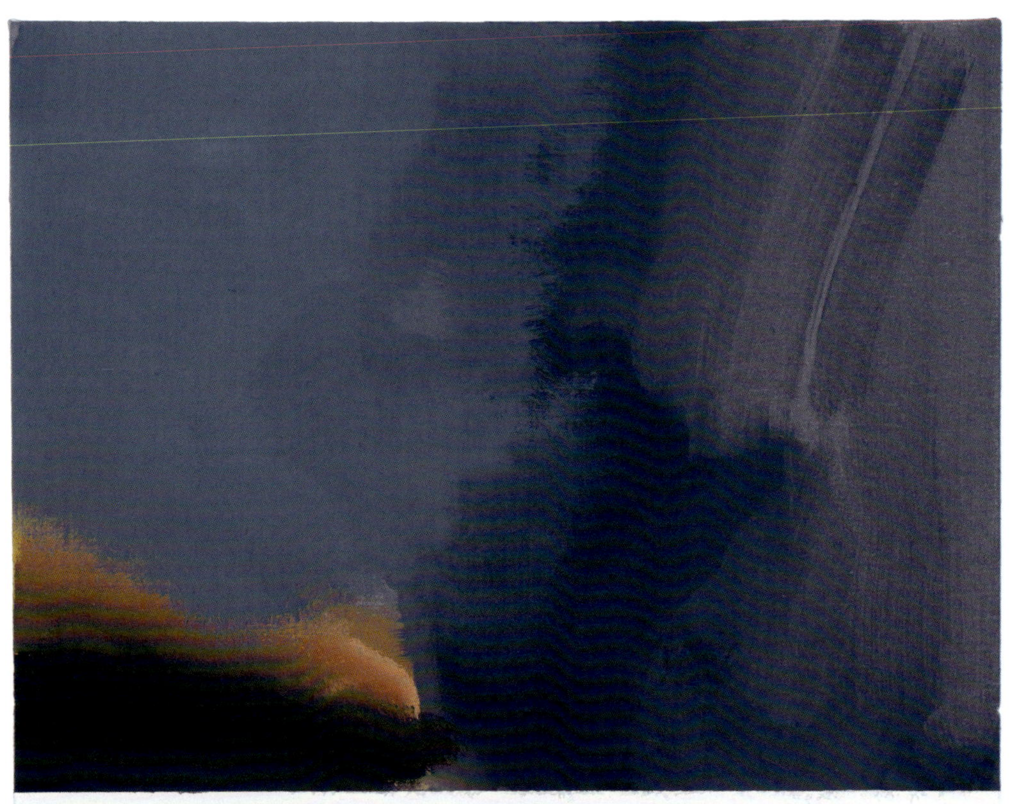

OCTOBER

S	M	T	W	Tr	F	Sa

NOVEMBER

S	M	T	W	Tr	F	Sa

DECEMBER

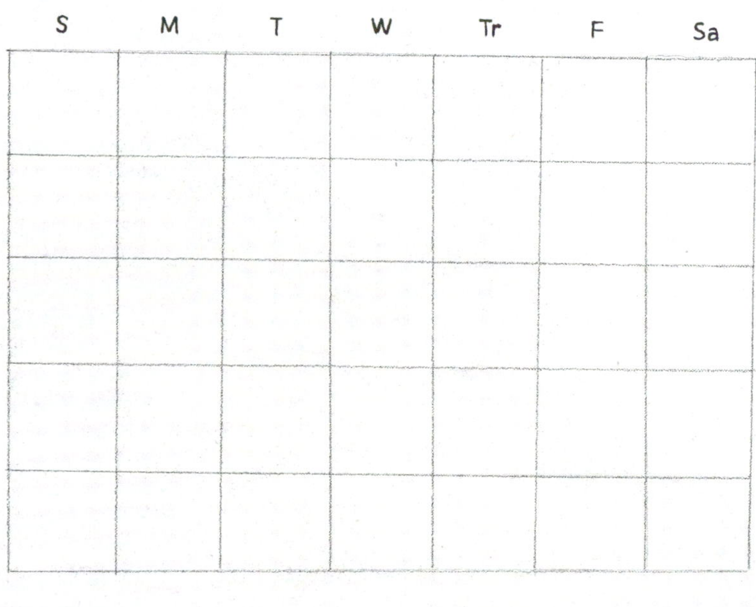

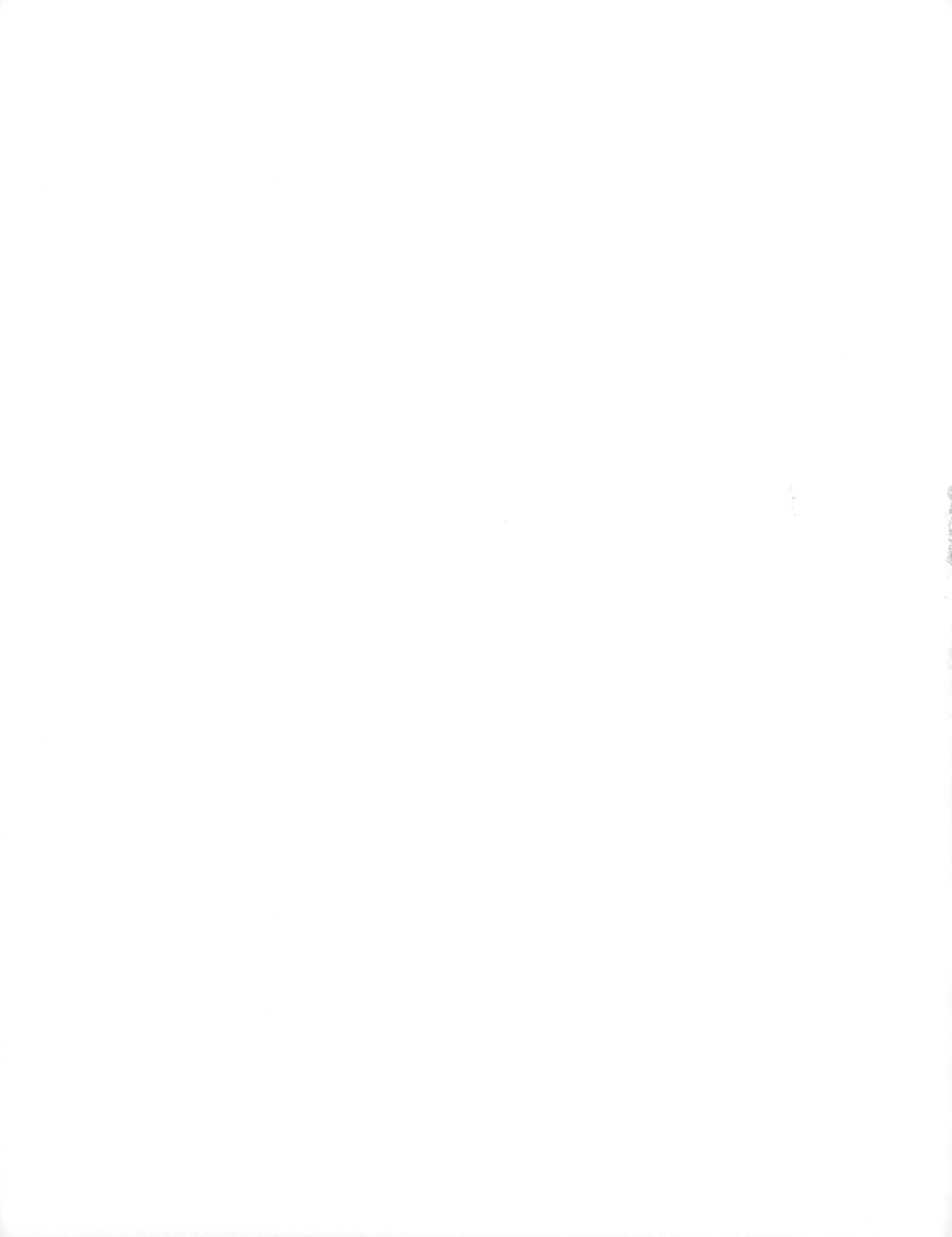

Study for Lid
2022
Watercolor, gouache, and
colored pencil on paper
10 ¾ × 8 ½ inches
27.3 × 21.6 cm

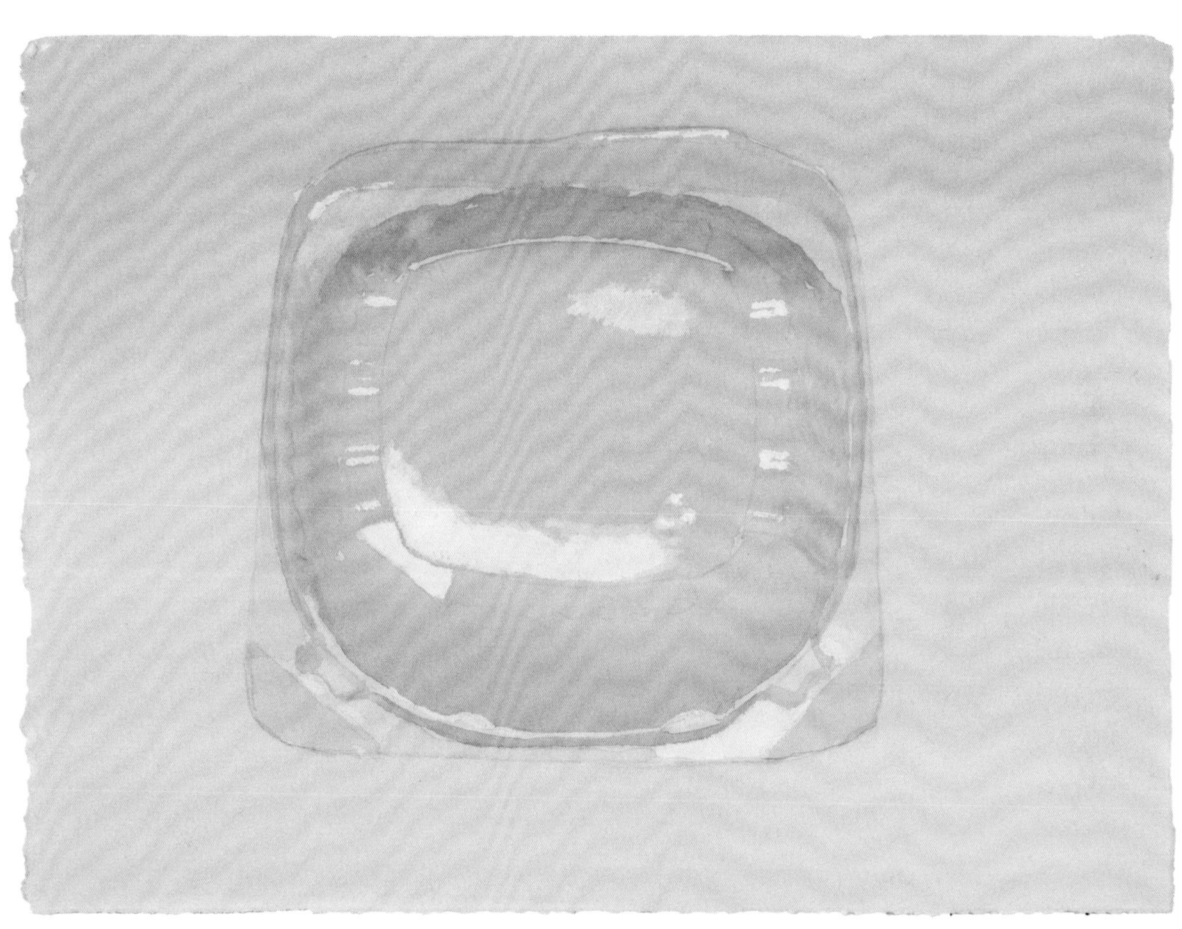

Beachgoers (I)
2024
Watercolor on paper
13 ½ × 9 inches
34.3 × 22.9 cm

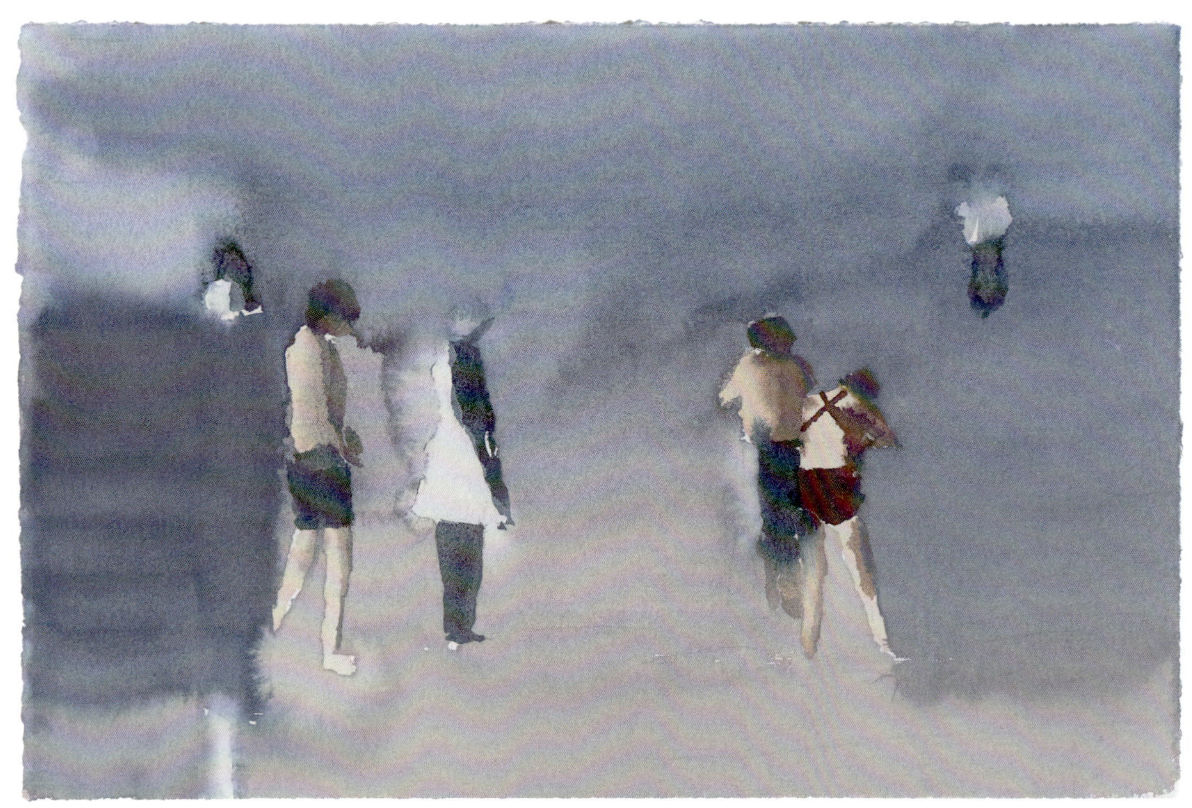

Beachgoers (II)
2024
Watercolor and colored pencil on paper
11 ¾ × 6 ¾ inches
29.9 × 15.2 cm

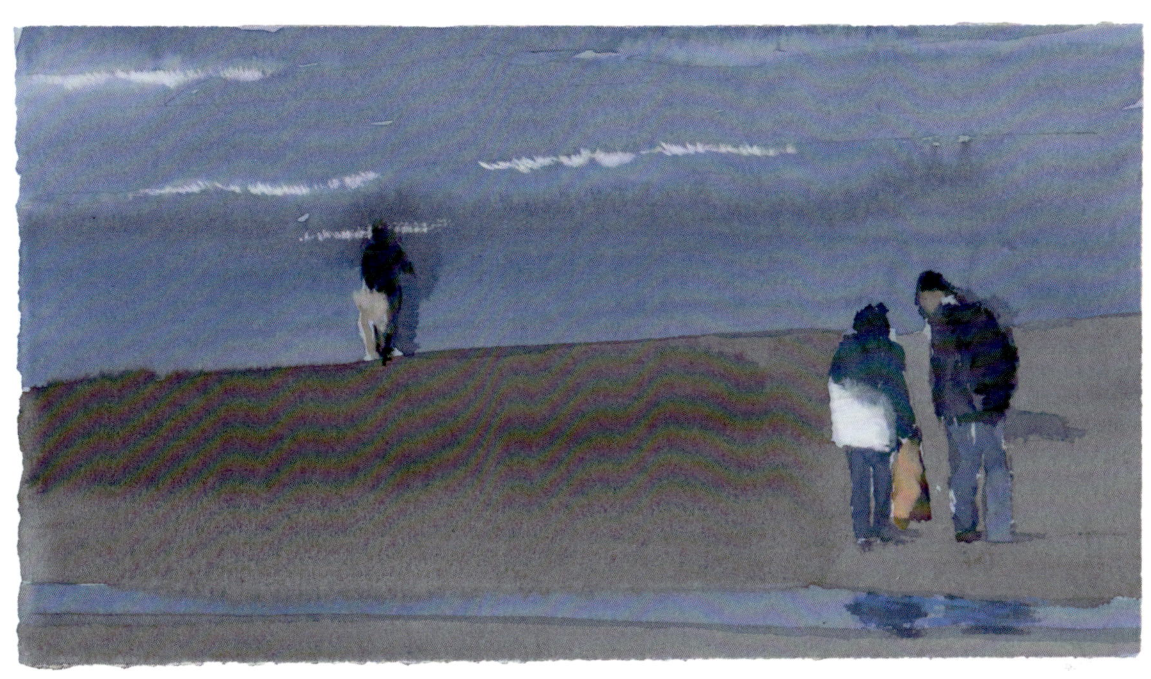

The whale, Mission Beach, NBC 7
2024
Watercolor and colored pencil on paper
12 × 9 ½ inches
30.5 × 24.1 cm

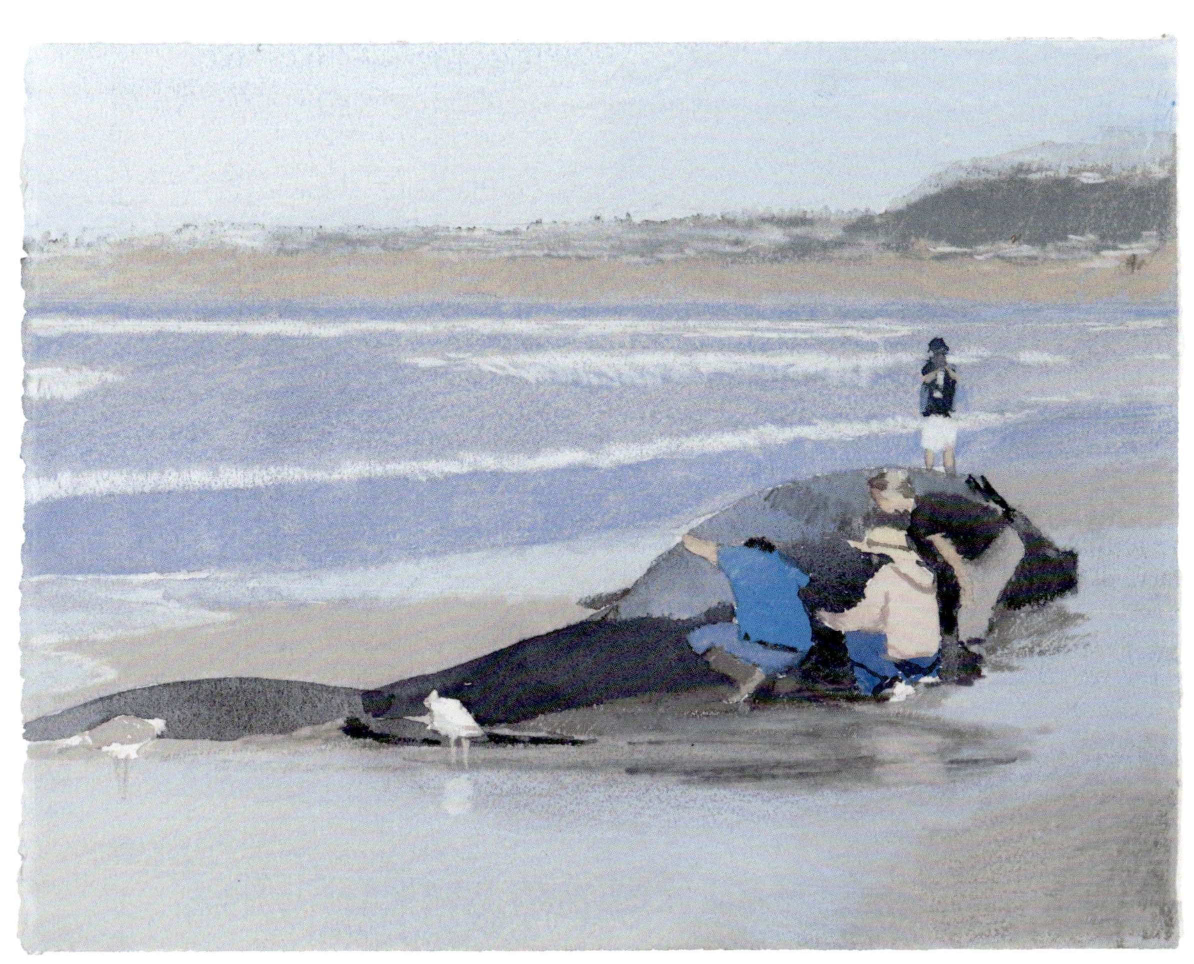

The Pool Sweeper
2022
Watercolor, gouache, and
colored pencil on paper
8 ¼ × 8 ½ inches
21 × 21.6 cm

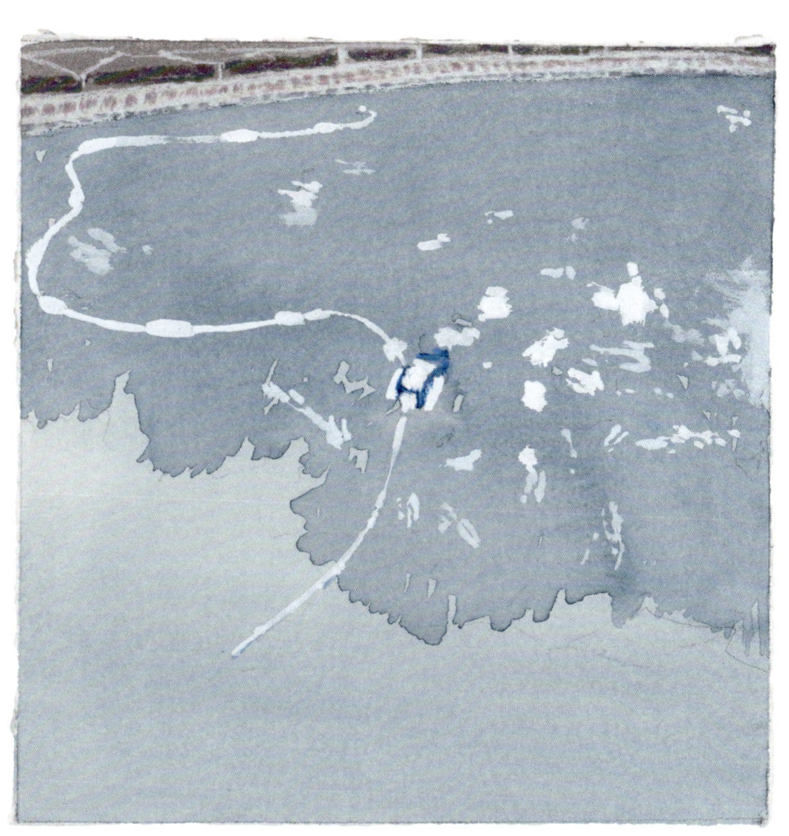

Man in Sand City
2023
Watercolor and colored pencil on paper
22 × 11½ inches
55.9 × 29.2 cm

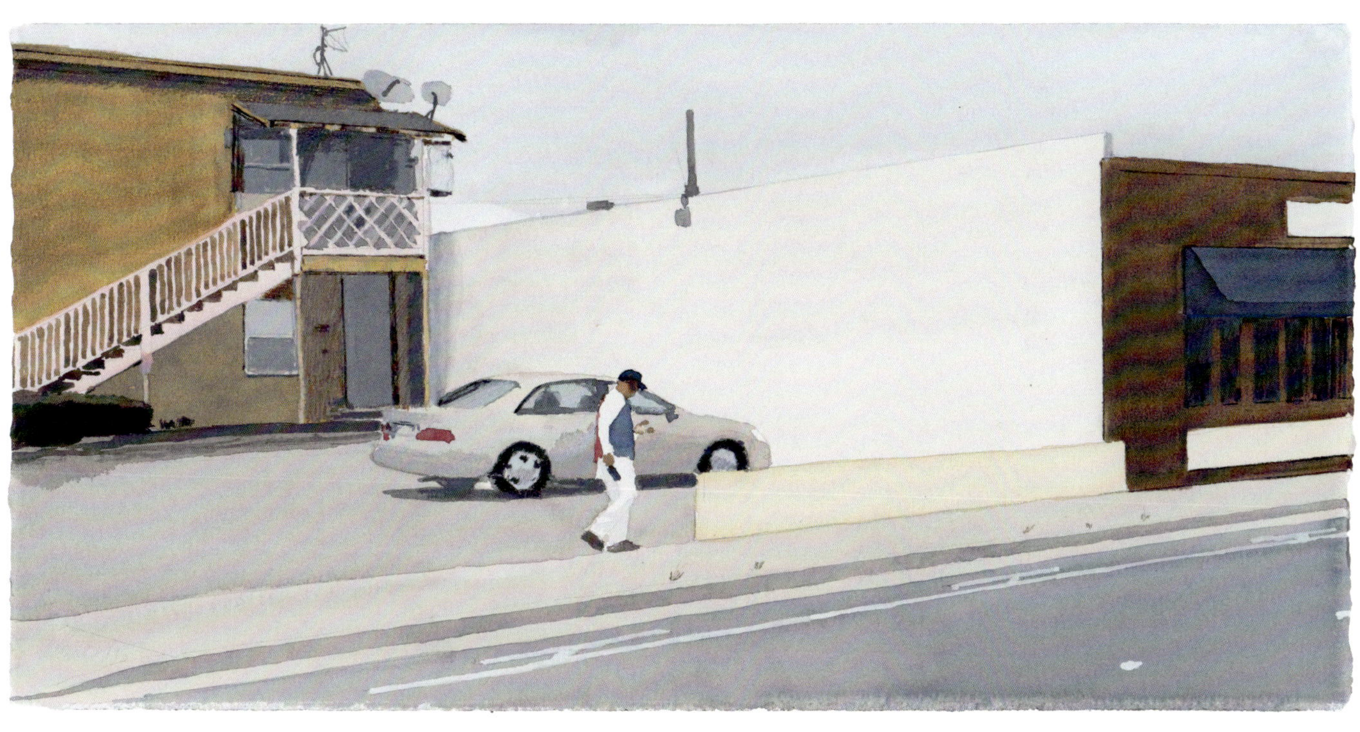

Study for Interstate
2023
Watercolor on paper
22 × 13 ¾ inches
55.9 × 34.9 cm

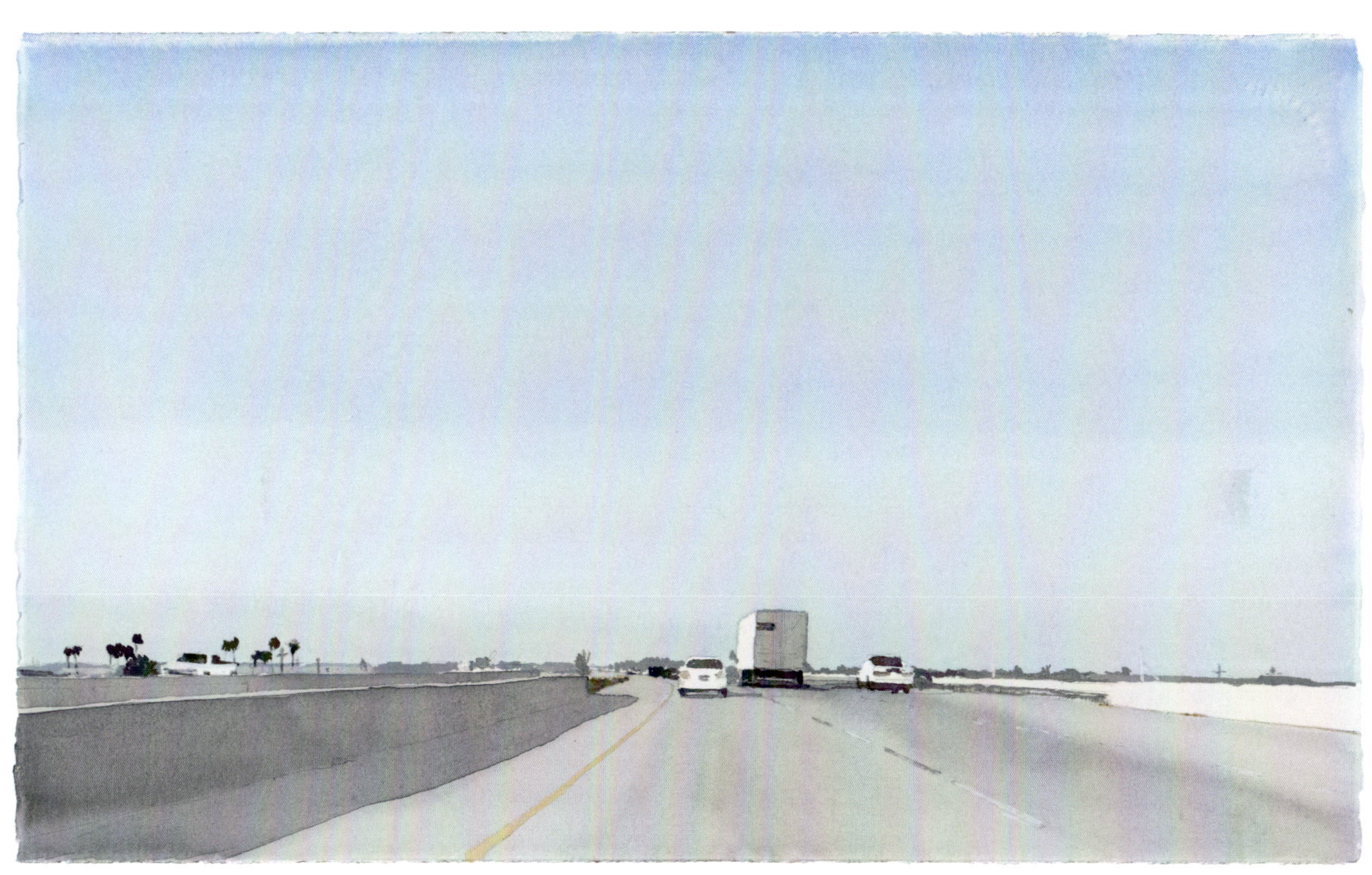

Seaside
2023–24
Watercolor, gouache, and
colored pencil on paper
17 ¾ × 12 inches
45 × 30.5 cm

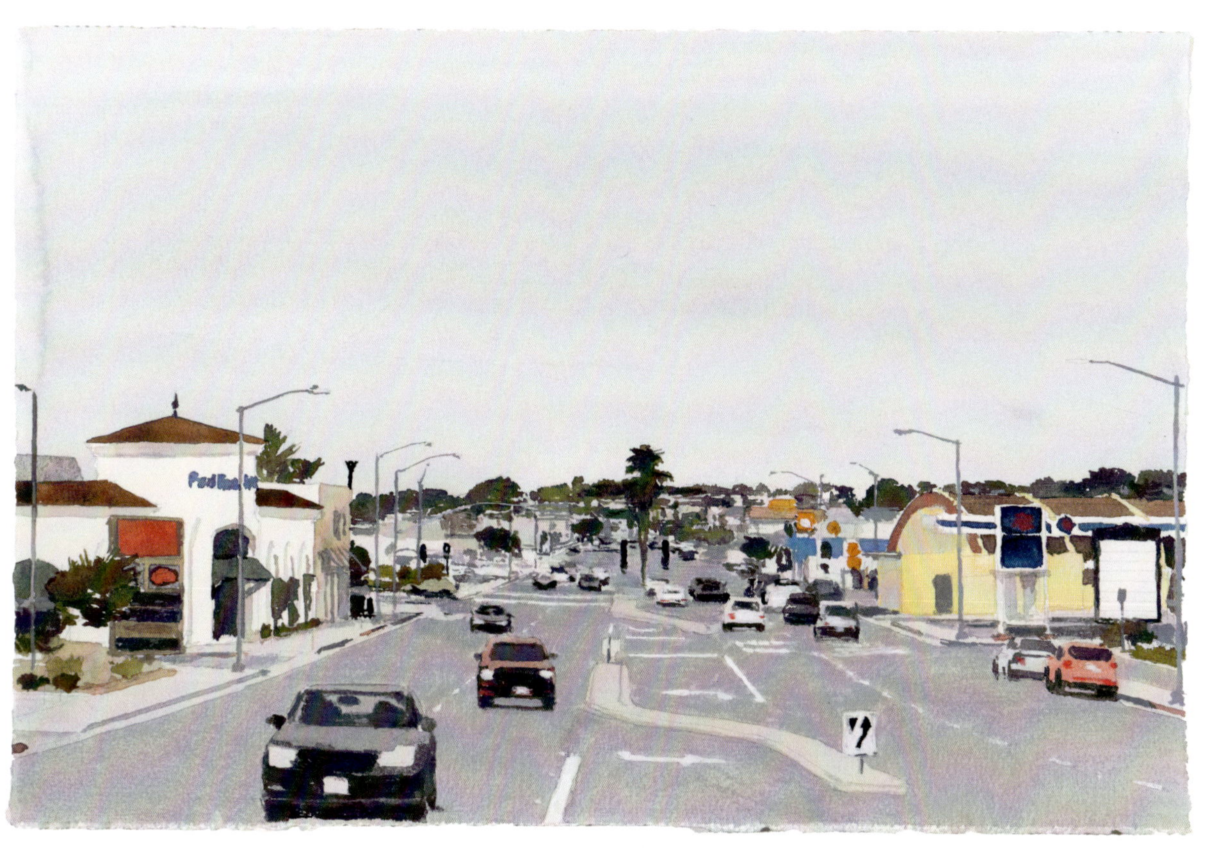

SBW
2024
Watercolor and colored pencil on paper
6 ¼ × 11 ½ inches
15.9 × 29.2 cm

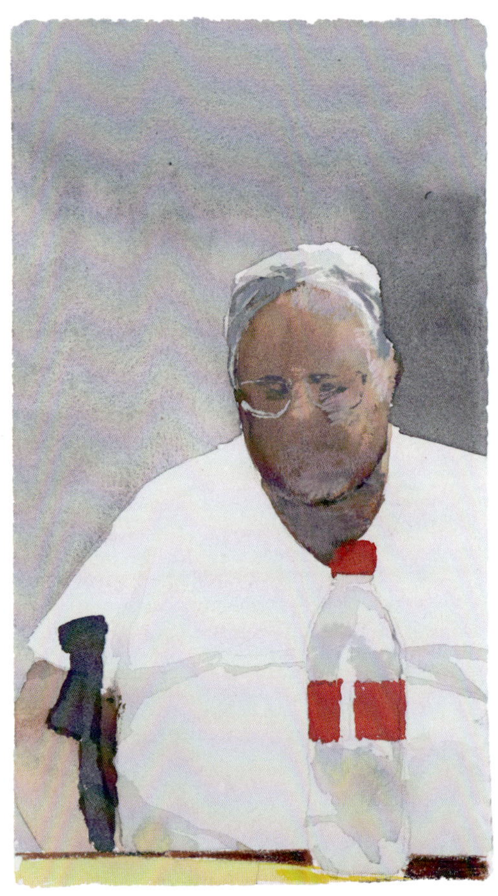

Ryan and Leon
2023
Watercolor and colored pencil on paper
8 × 11½ inches
20.3 × 29.2 cm

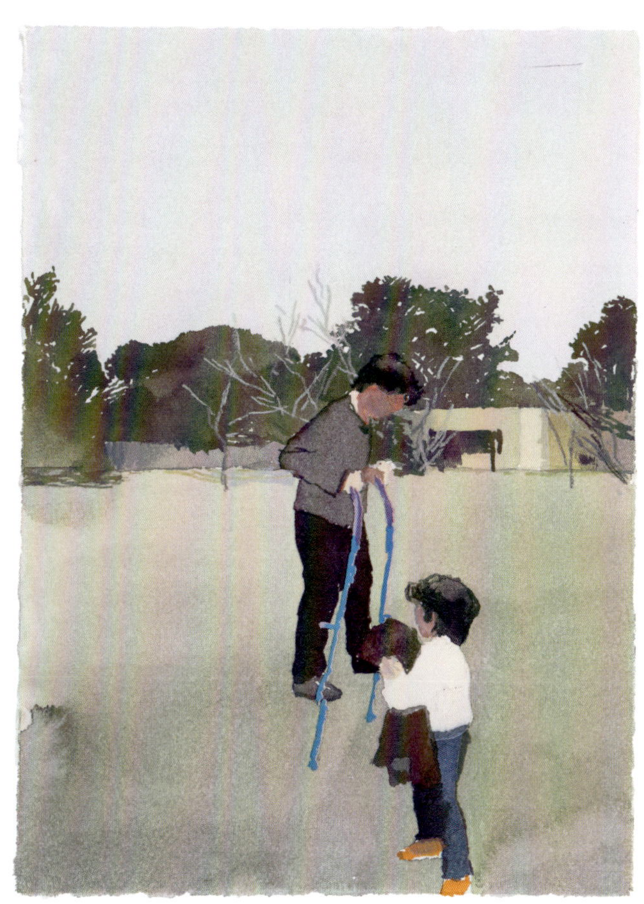

Motel room in Redwood City
2023
Watercolor and colored pencil on paper
13 ¾ × 10 inches
34.9 × 25.4 cm

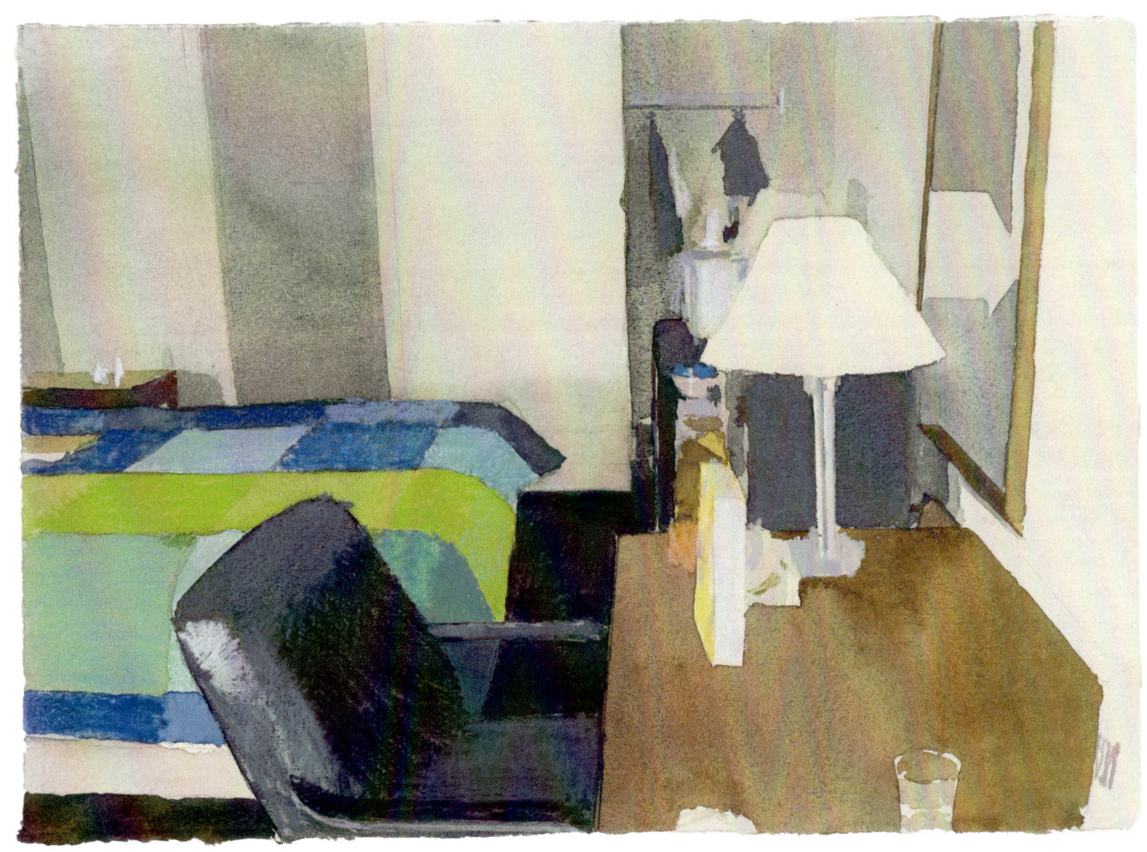

LA
2024
Watercolor and colored pencil on paper
7 ¾ × 9 ¼ inches
19.7 × 23.5 cm

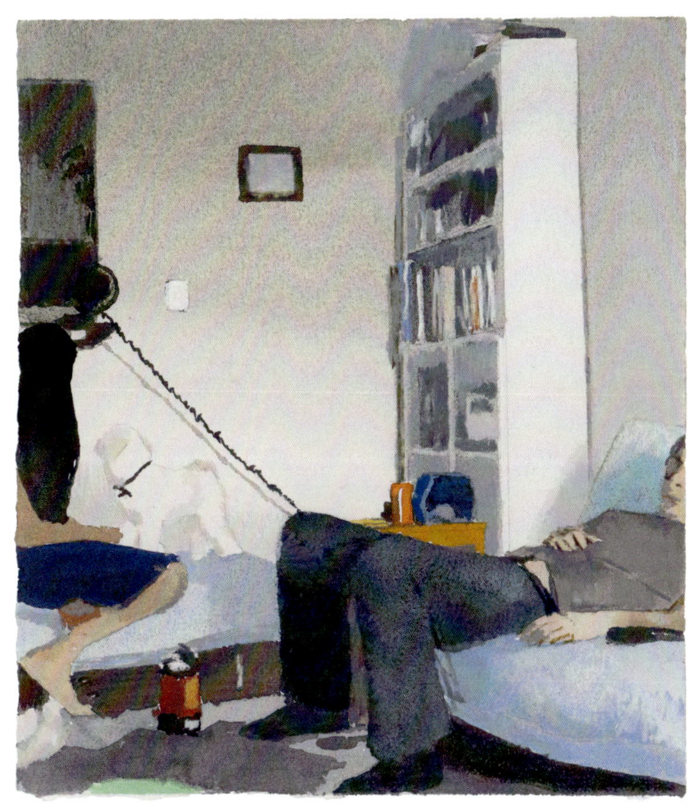

Sunflower
2024
Watercolor on paper
18 ¾ × 14 ¼ inches
47.6 × 36.2 cm

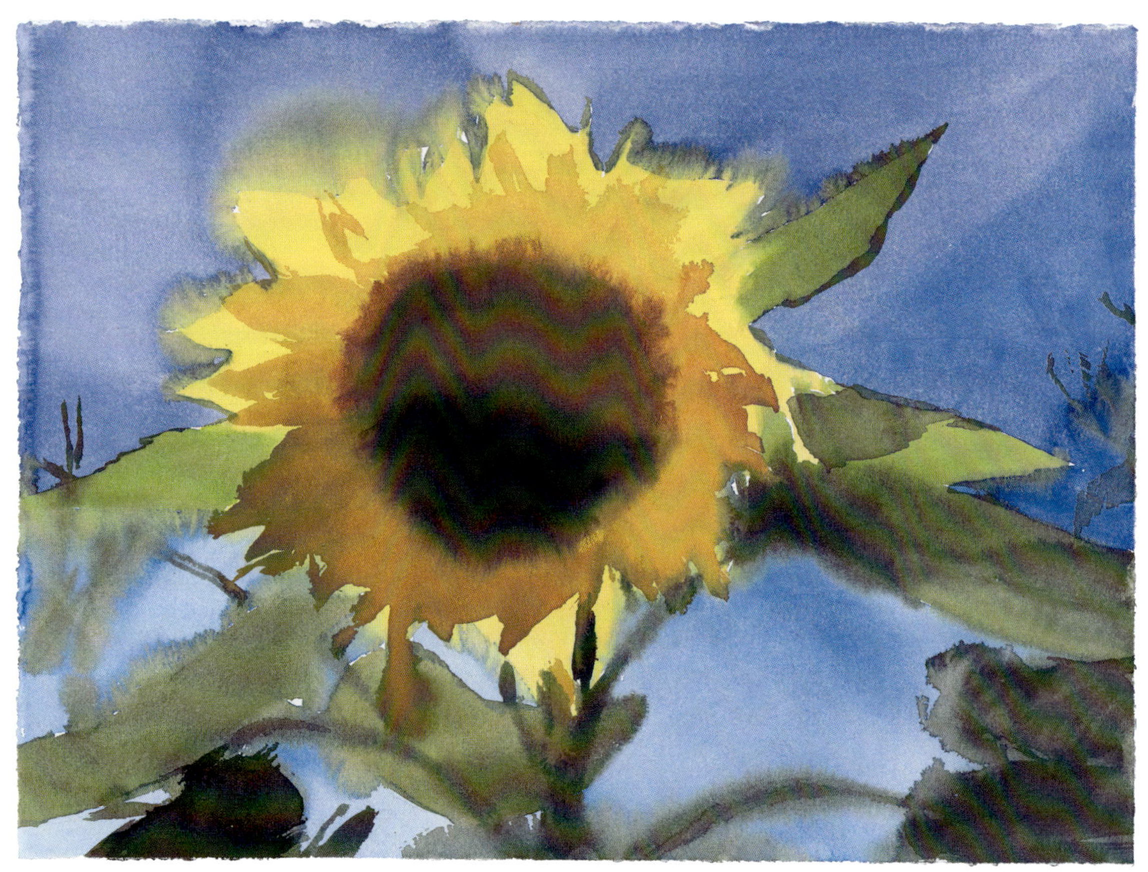

Walking
2023
Watercolor and colored pencil on paper
10 ¾ × 15 ¾ inches
27.3 × 14.6 cm

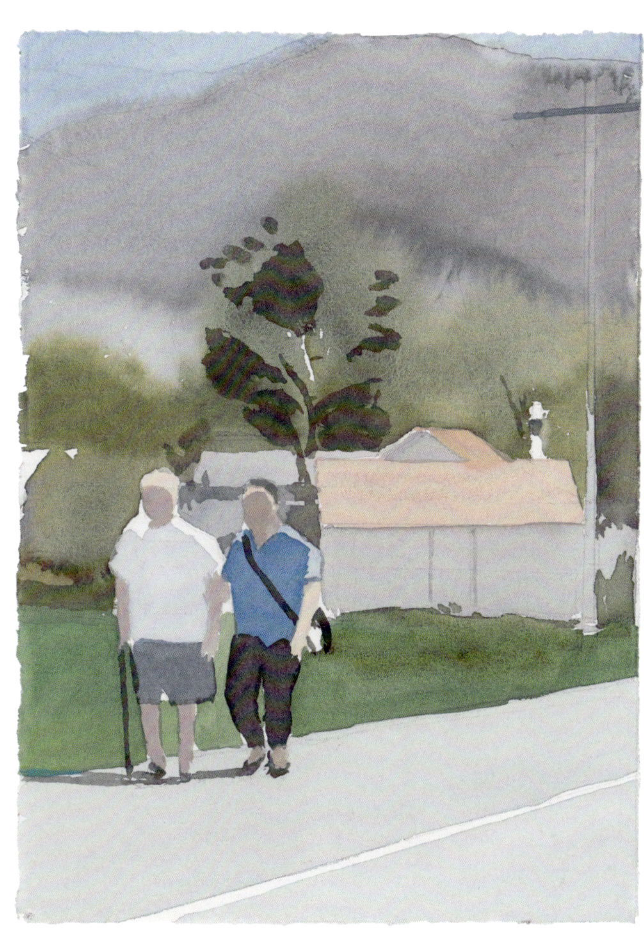

Portrait of the artist's mother from the roof of his childhood home
2022
Watercolor and colored pencil on paper
10 ½ × 8 ½ inches
26.7 × 21.6 cm

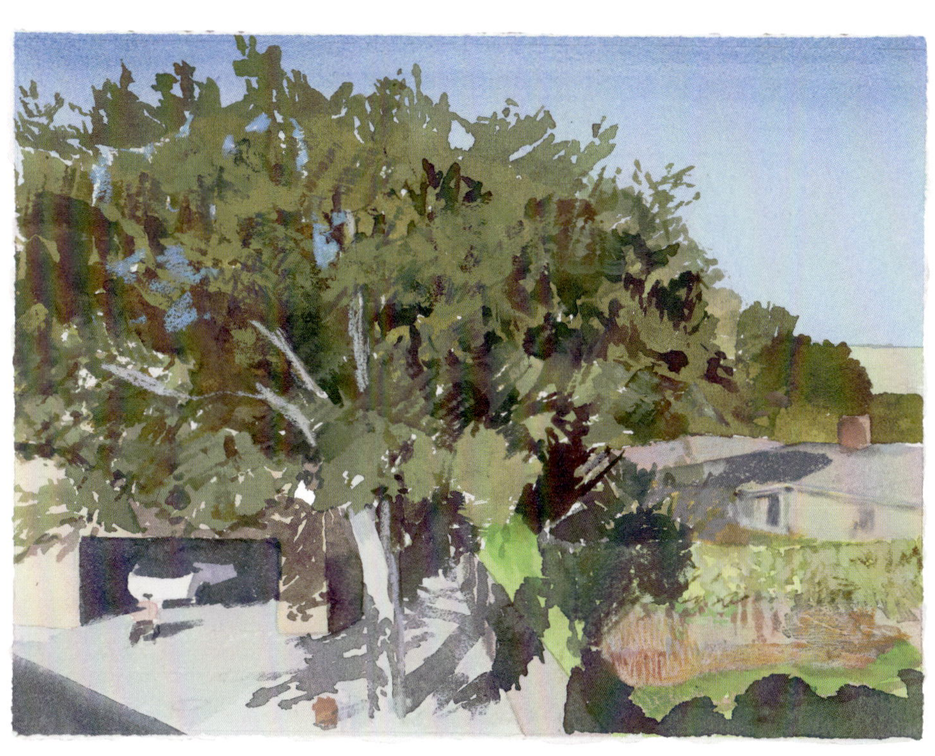

Paper Flowers, Monterey (III)
2023
Watercolor and colored pencil on paper
15 × 11 inches
38.1 × 27.9 cm

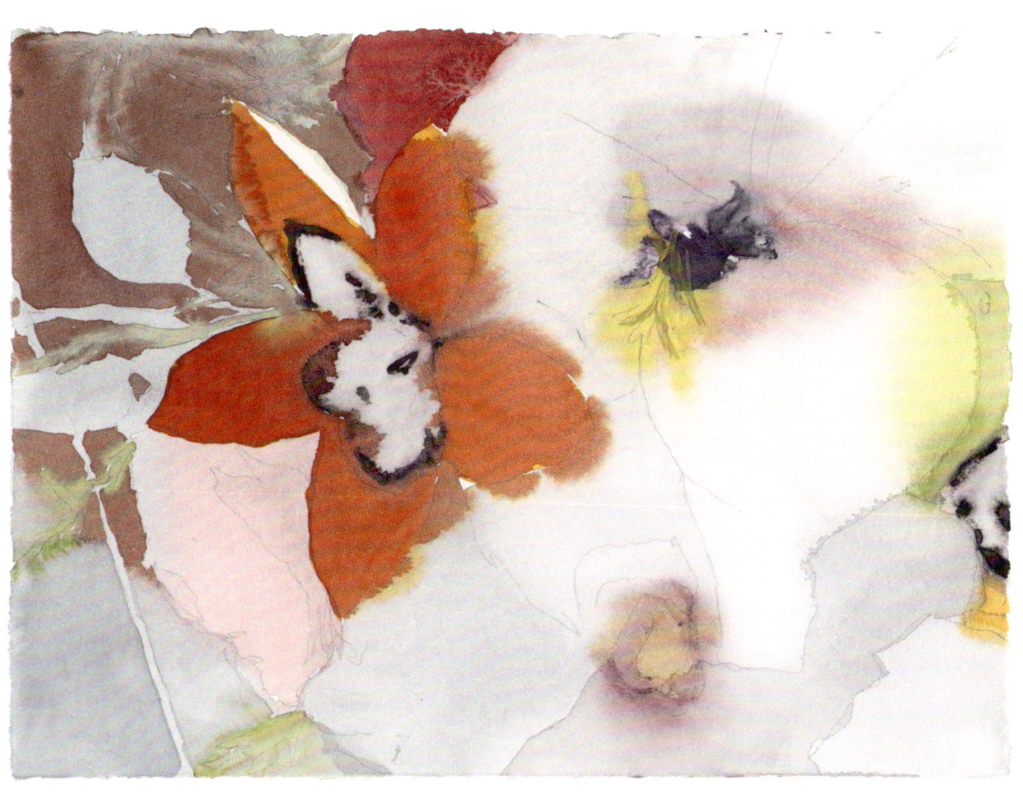

Brita
2022
Watercolor and colored pencil on paper
14 ¼ × 14 ¼ inches
36.2 × 36.2 cm

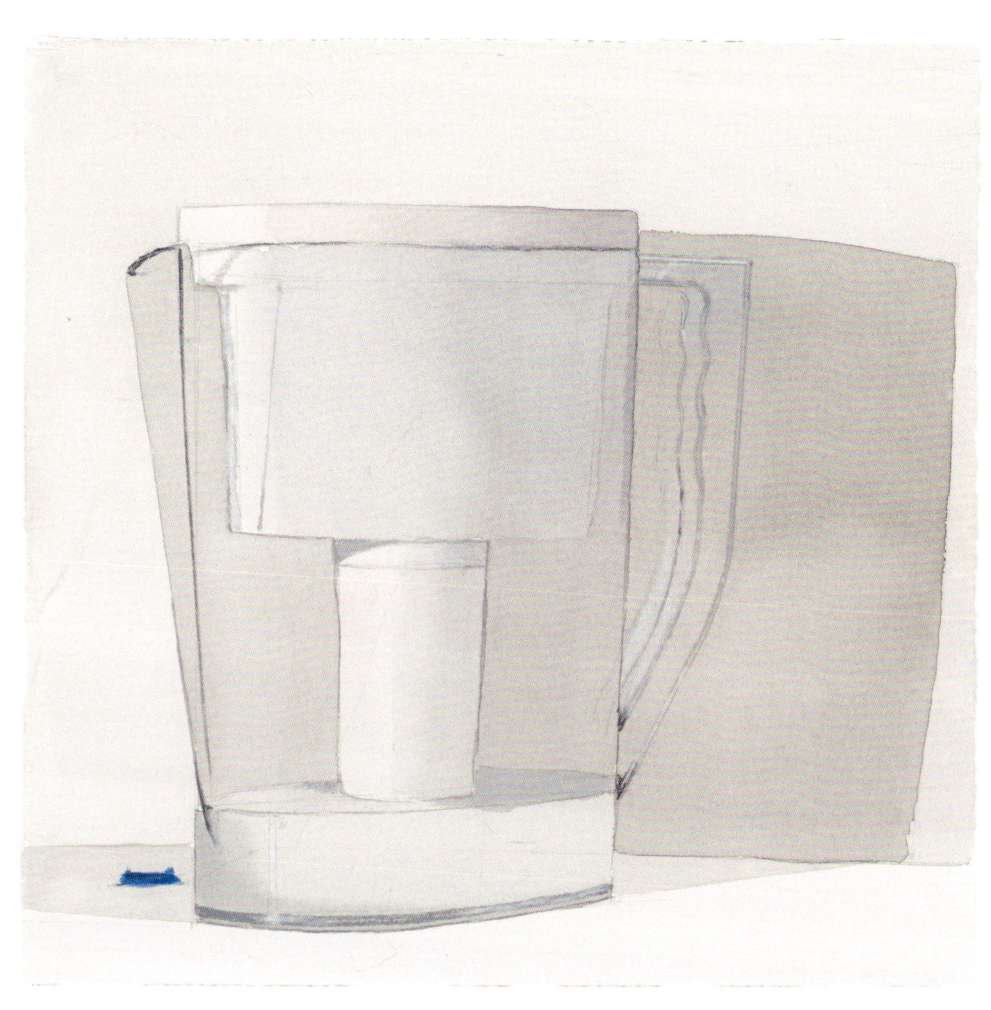

Tissue Box
2016
Watercolor and colored pencil on paper
12 × 8 ¼ inches
30.5 × 21 cm

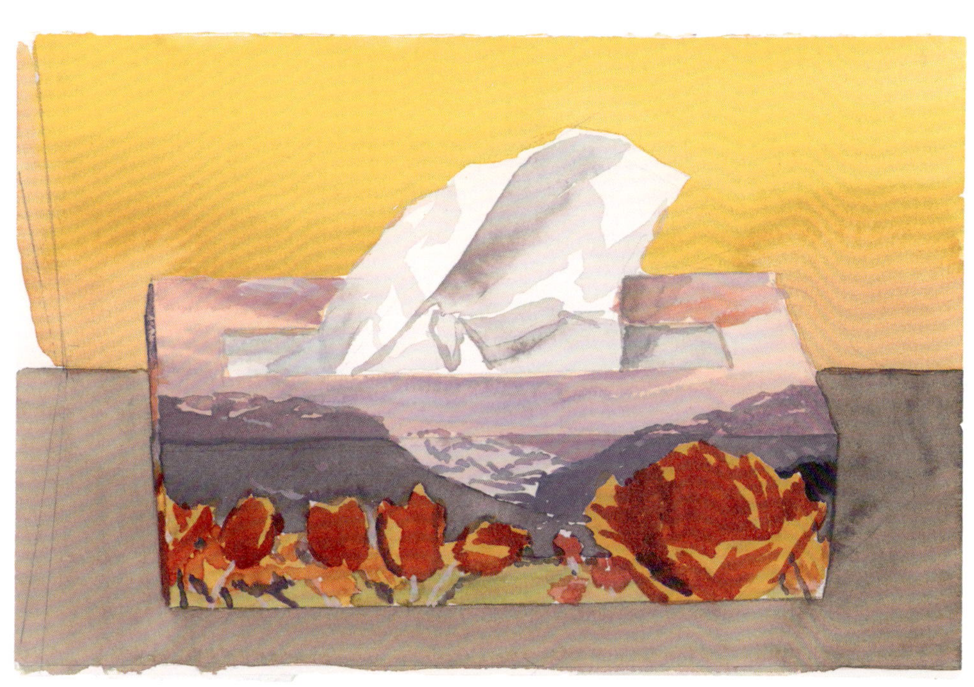

Container (II)
2020
Oil on linen
20 × 16 inches
50.8 × 40.6 cm

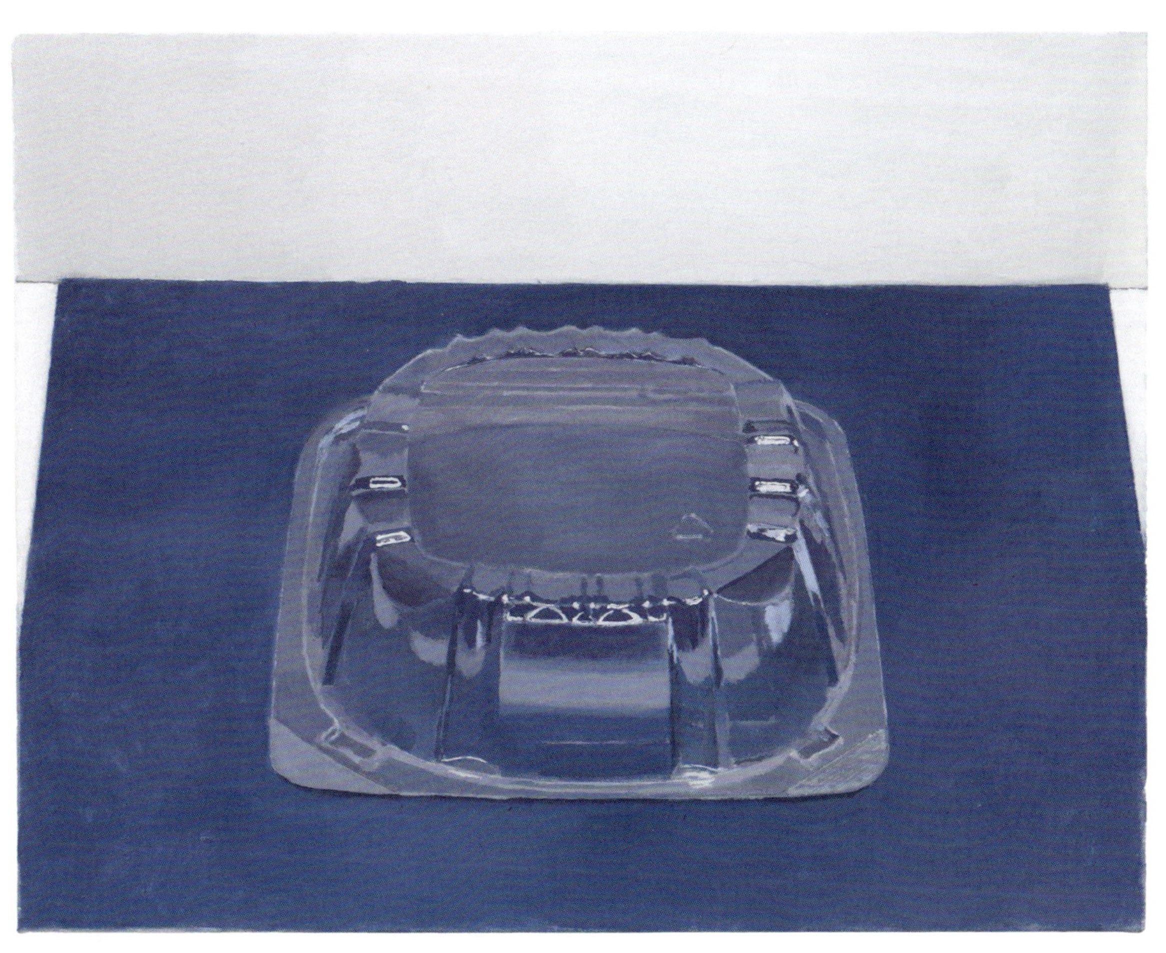

Container (III)
2020
Oil on linen
24 × 22 inches
61 × 55.9 cm

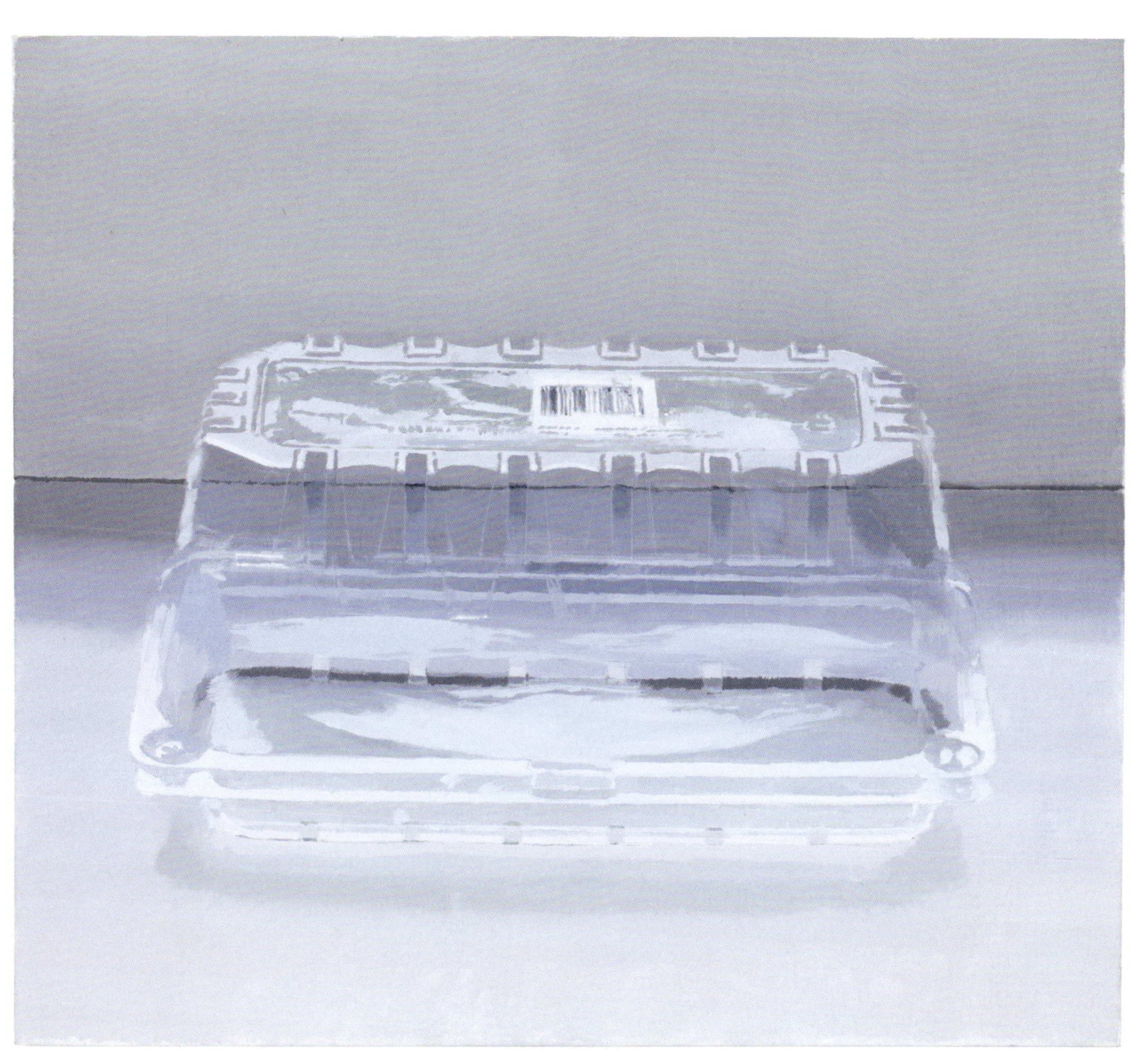

Untitled (Maggie orchids)
2014
Oil on canvas
12 × 16 inches
30.5 × 40.6 cm

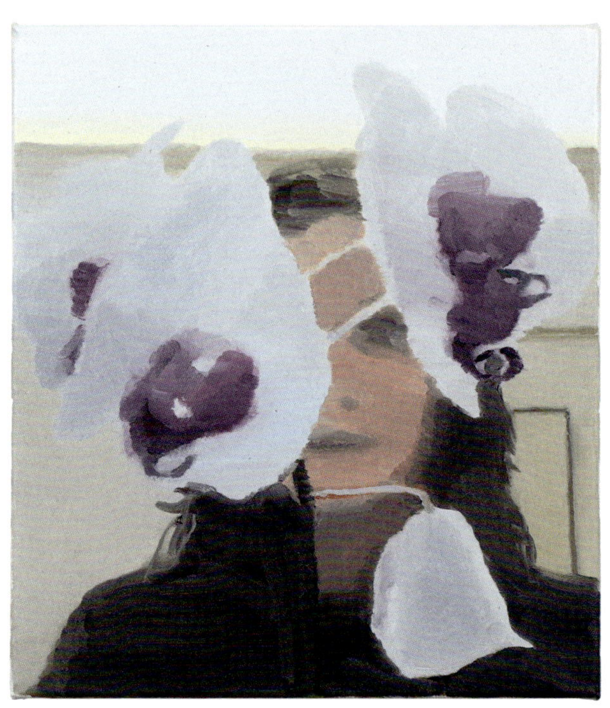

Interior Painter
2015
Oil on canvas
28 × 20 inches
71.1 × 50.8 cm

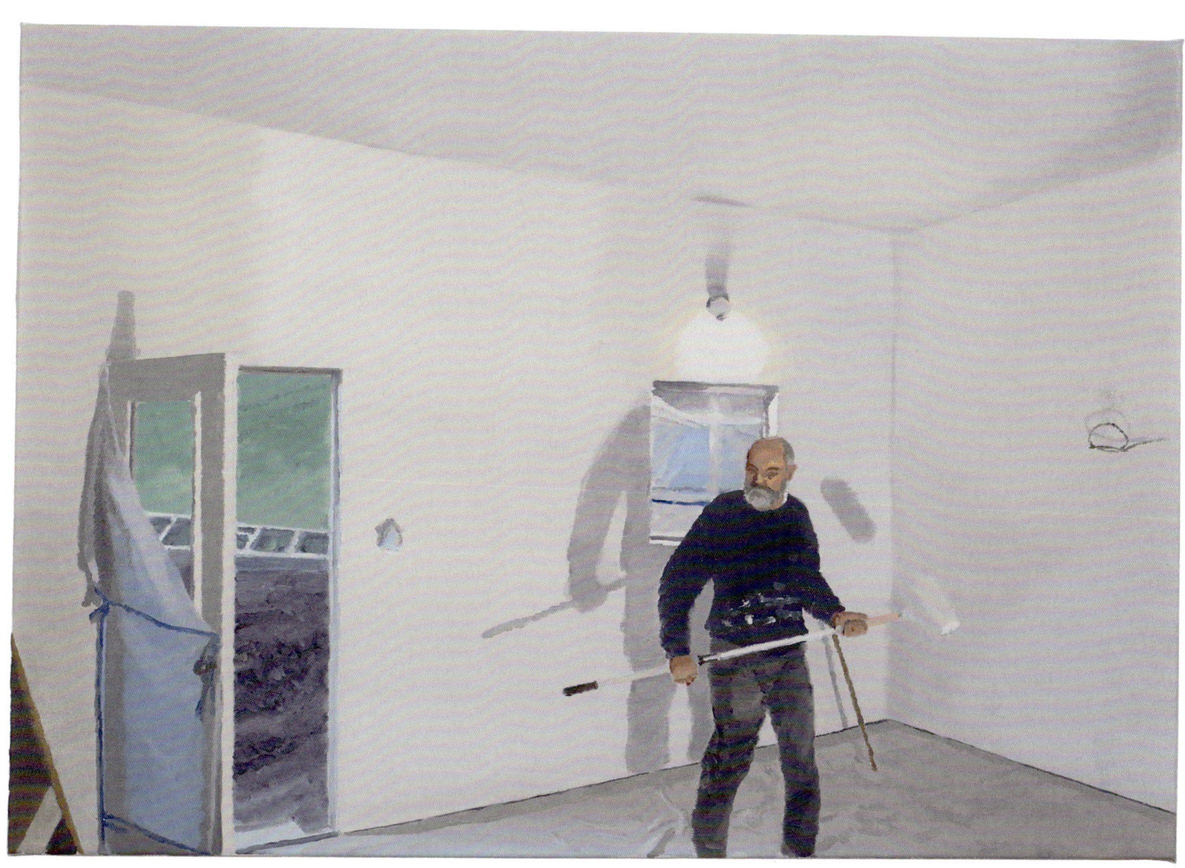

Large Sun
2015
Acylic on canvas
92 × 66 inches
233.7 × 167.6 cm

October 2027
2021
Oil on linen
14 × 22 inches
35.6 × 55.9 cm

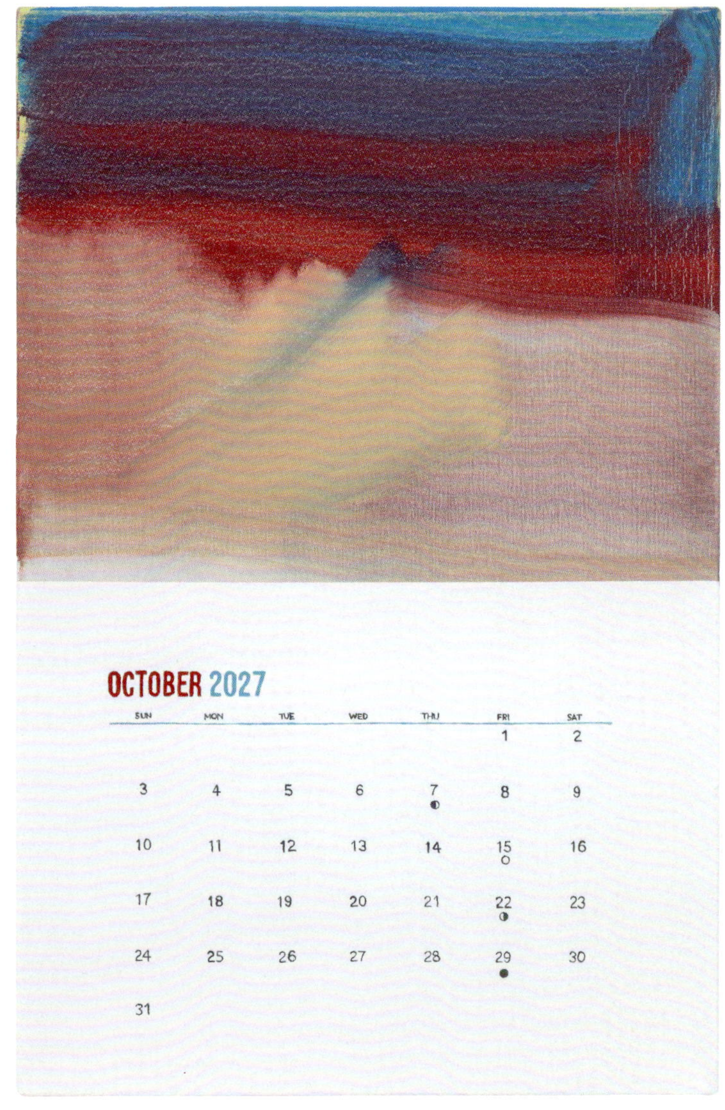

Hottest and coldest places, August 18, 2021
2021
Oil on linen
14 × 22 inches
35.6 × 55.9 cm

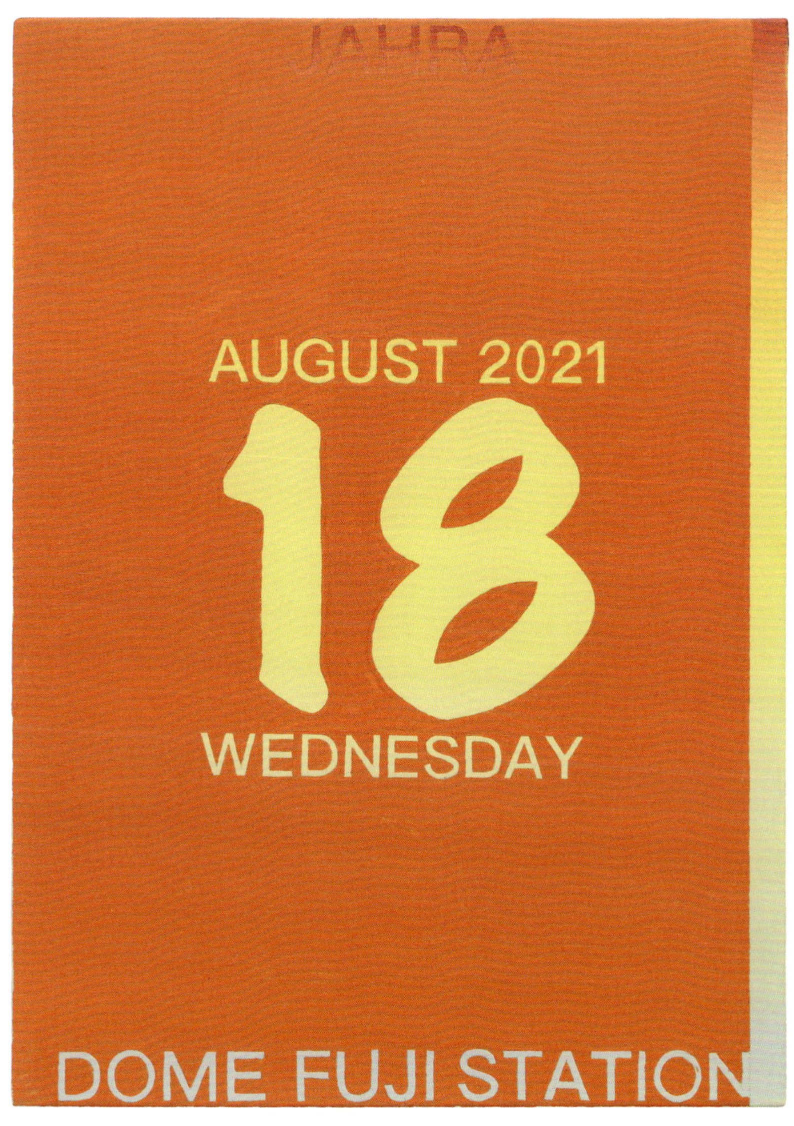

Palms
2018
Oil on linen
33 × 33 inches
83.8 × 83.8 cm

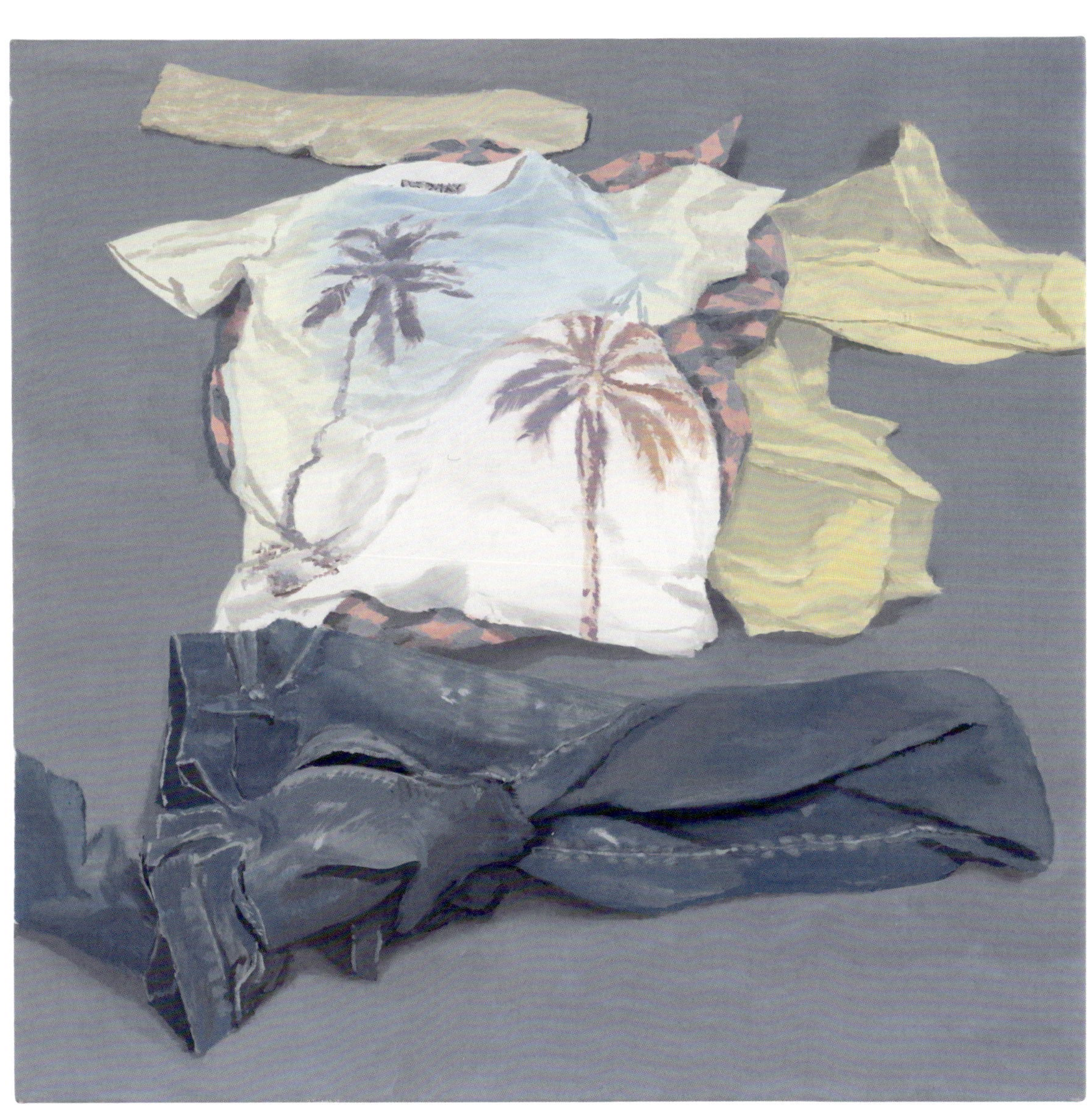

Pitcher and flowers
2018
Oil on linen
20 × 22 inches
50.8 × 55.9 cm

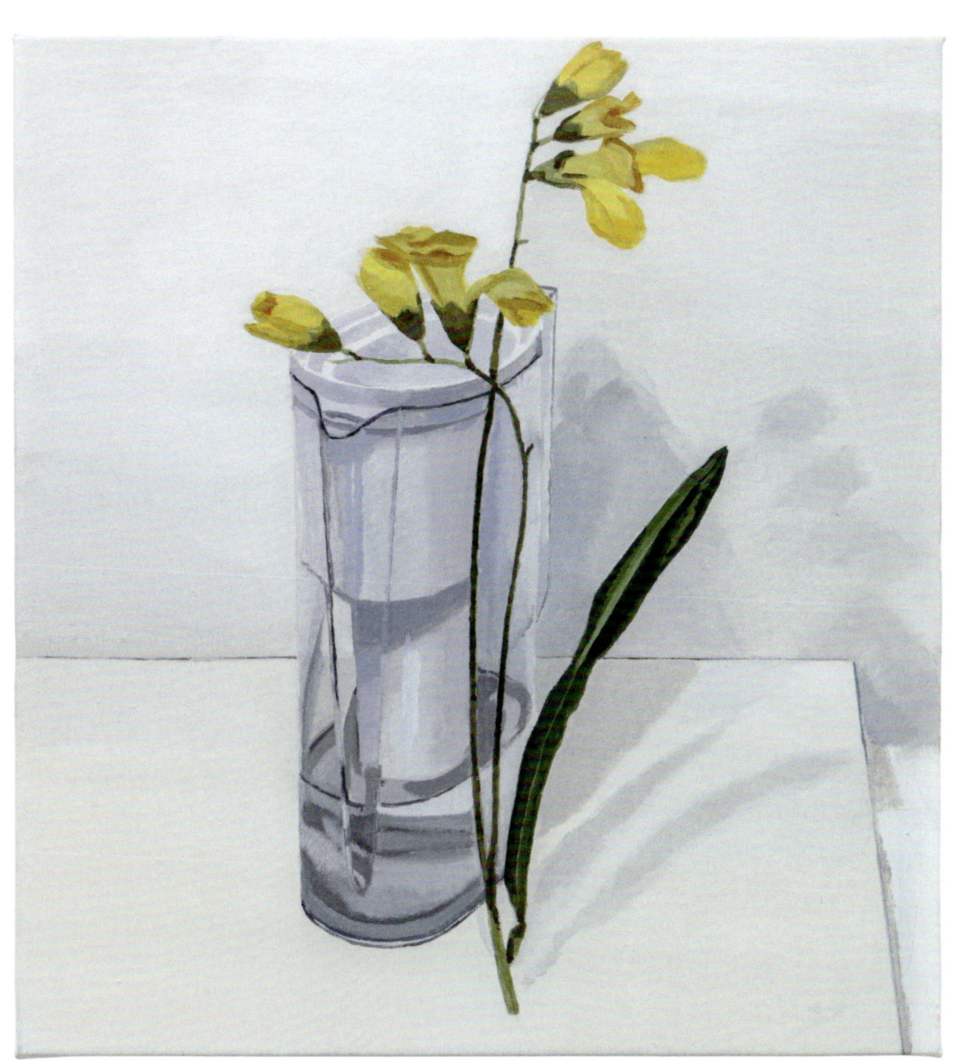

Untitled (round mirror)
2015
Oil on linen
20 × 18 inches
50.8 × 45.7 cm

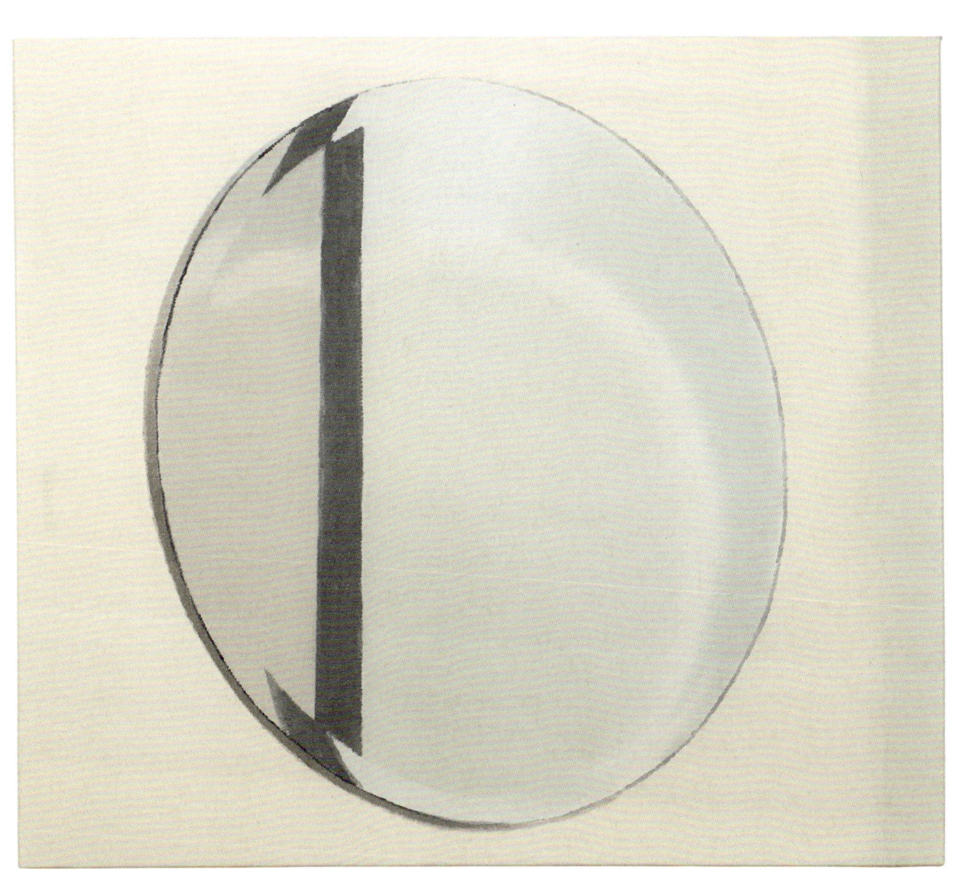

The Compost
2018
Oil on linen
15 × 13 inches
38.1 × 33 cm

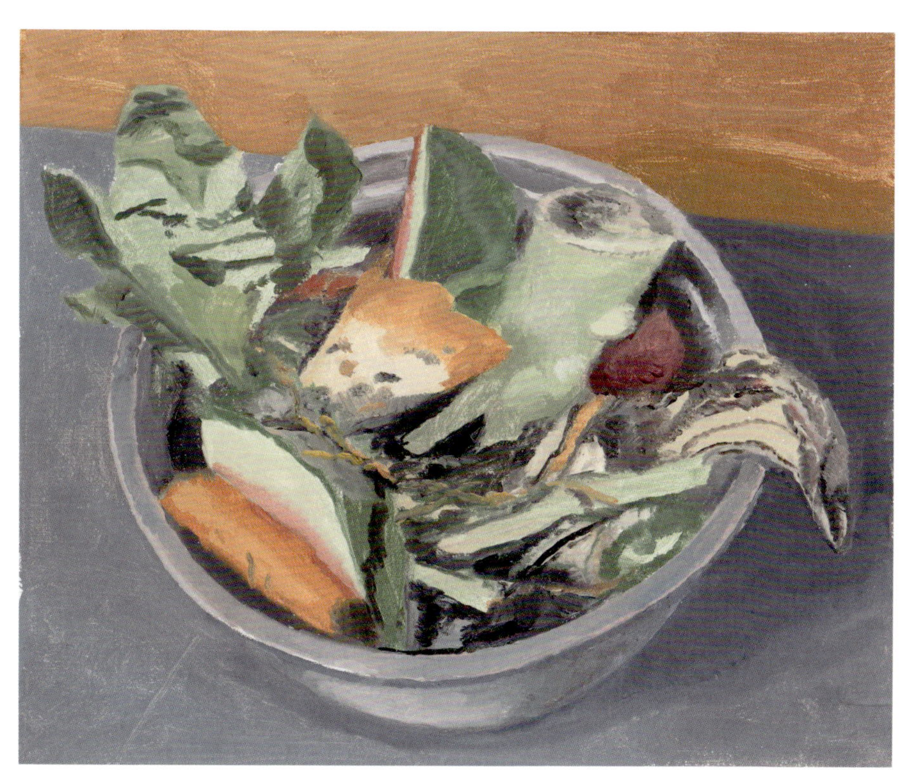

Picture Time

Ross Simonini

Humans want to see time, to give it shape.

We imagine time as a relentless force. We bargain with it and race against it, and as the visual beings we are, we want to look our rival in the eye. We want to transform this abstract idea into reality so that we might heal our endless anxiety about the future.

Science views time through physics. Newton described it as a container and Einstein folded it into space. Time is measured in observable movement—a day is a turn of the earth; a year, an orbit around the sun.

For millennia, time has been a circle—the wheel of samsara, the Maya calendar, Nietzsche's eternal return.

The sundial materialized this. The clock mechanized it. The watch bound it to our bodies. We even named it "watch" because wherever we go, we keep our gaze fixed upon the second hand as it ticks away our lives.

The most common image of time is the simplest: a straight line. Invented in 1765, the timeline is a track in a single direction.

Soon came synchronized times and the age of punctuality began: time zones, railroad time, consensual time.

In a famous debate with Einstein, the philosopher Henri Bergson rejected the whole paradigm of spatial time for an intuitive temporal experience. True time, he said, can only be accessed through introspection, and he called this phenomenon "duration." Duration is the time produced by humans, rather than observed by them—a creative force, not a metric.

Bergson lost the debate, so we live in Einstein time, but he inspired many artists with his ideas, most notably Marcel Proust, whose *In Search of Lost Time* was an opus of duration.

Humans are aware of our personal time. We are morning larks, night owls, nostalgics, worrywarts. *Can you believe a whole year has already passed? I thought that week would never end.*

Bergson believed that if we come to know our own duration, we become filled with genius and produce something truly new.

Paint Time

Marcel Duchamp's *Nude Descending a Staircase* illustrated space time by recalling the blurry, time-lapsed images of chronophotography. But most art expresses time in less literal terms.

Unlike space time, which can be shown in symbols, duration cannot be reduced to a universal image and all art contains its own duration.

Literature invents its own relationship to time. Writers bend the pacing of plot to suit the needs of their ideas. Jorge Luis Borges saw his work as inventing "an infinite series of times ... parallel times ... a network of times."

The filmmaker Chantal Akerman spoke of wanting to capture "the physical experience of time unfolding inside you."

The interdisciplinary artist Dieter Roth spoke of using his work to record "a moment that endures ... that remains embedded and suspended in time."

Art objects appear static, although we know they are not. Perhaps this is why fine art prioritizes timelessness, while fashion, film, and pop music emphasize trends and technology.

Timelessness is unreal but it is a suspension of disbelief that allows painting to invent new temporal possibilities. This is the enchantment of picture time.

Anyone who has ever lived with art knows how paint reveals itself over time. Every hour and mood transforms the work. After years of looking, a fresh shadow appears beneath a foot. The paint cracks like aged skin, offering its color back to the sun.

Some paintings explode on first look; others enter the eyes in an instant but remain quietly hanging in the mind for weeks, releasing their potency in a slow drip.

A work may take twenty years before a viewer is ready to receive it. Each artwork and viewer form their own temporal relationship.

Present Time

For me, duration is among of the great sensations of art. A good picture activates our sense of sight, space, body, and time. It dissolves the linear, circular diagrams and presents us with a direct metaphysical experience.

Roger White is a painter of duration. Through the classic forms—landscapes, still lifes, domestic scenes—he offers a doorway into the passage of time. When I look at his pictures, the clock fades away and I discover the rate of my nervous system.

There is no drama in these paintings. Emotional stimulation blurs time: on bad days, time drags, and on good ones it flies. For an artist, time speeds up when work is going well and stagnates when inspiration flags. The same could be said for viewing art. A bad film lasts forever.

Of course, a life free of conflict is neither possible nor desirable, but when art like White's offers a respite from drama, we are given the opportunity to see beyond our mood, beyond the mechanical clock and peer into our own duration.

In spiritual practices, it is sacred to commune with time. Some call it "the now" or "God." A seeker might reach for this communion through prayer or meditation and when she arrives there, it is said that she discovers the apotheosis of consciousness.

White gives the viewer glimpses of this awareness through objects so unremarkable they seem to bypass stimulation—a Brita water jug, a toilet bowl. He calls this the "presence" of painting.

Presence is a challenging state. There's immediate pleasure in stimulation and distraction, but presence is a more subtle phenomenon. People who want to deeply connect with the present move to mountaintops and monasteries. They spend years sloughing off emotional noise and perceptual ticks.

Truly knowing time, or anything or anyone, is complex. An art experience of time is no different.

When I look at one of Roger White's watercolors—a sprawling urban landscape in the late afternoon—I somehow feel resentment, melancholy, clarity, and wonder all at once. It's a little overwhelming, but along with all these feelings, White offers the sublime. The beauty of the world can save us from ourselves.

Hand Time

Time is a fundamental medium for artists. Some pictures take years to create, some seconds. A line can be drawn in a swipe or a drag. A mark in space is a mark in time.

The tempo of perceiving a painting might come from the pace of its creation: a Joan Mitchell flings itself at me; an Agnes Martin draws me in; a Helen Frankenthaler pours into my eyes.

The vocation of painting is also a game of time. "There's never enough time to paint," White says, "I hate that I wish I had more time to paint."

A "productive" artist uses time for production, but some painting requires hours of staring. And each medium has its temporal necessities. Tempera dries quickly. Terracota crumbles. Bronze lives forever. Roger White chooses slow-drying mediums: oil paint is a waiting game and watercolor is an evaporating puddle.

"I remember seeing a show of portraits by Hans Memling at the Frick," White says, "and thinking that there is not enough time in the modern world for someone to paint even *one finger* of one of these Flemish bankers. The entire structure of our experience is so radically different."

Ultimately, what humans desire is not more minutes, but the feeling that we used our time well. We did the best we could with the time we had.

All Time

White's mention of Memling invokes another category: historical time. Lineage, influence—these are sticky subjects for artists.

White works in the history of luminous painters: Caravaggio, Vermeer, Turner,

Yuskavage. Like them, he makes sunlight from paint.

He paints portraits of the sun, the ancient clock that helps to set our circadian rhythms.

Most still life painting is a portrait of the sun. A bowl of cherries allows me to feel the sun as it inches across the sky. It brings me to the present, where I am neither rushing nor waiting, only growing aware of my awareness.

I am experiencing the moment while forming a memory of the moment at the same time. This is how Bergson described déjà vu.

White Time

For me, White's calendar paintings are experiments with time. He depicts *the* diagram of modern time: the Gregorian calendar. It is a grid, intended to be read like a letter: left to right, top to bottom.

He stretches us into speculative time by creating years from the future—2049, 2086, 2027. He embeds abstract paintings inside the calendars themselves, creating paintings within paintings, times within times.

The more I consider White's work through time, the more I see it in his fundamental impulse as an artist. His mirror paintings, his empty rooms, his studies of plastic packaging.

"When I talk about the plastic container paintings," White says, "I mention that there are lots of implicit time scales: the time it takes to make the object, the time it takes to use it, the time it takes me to make the painting, a duration that the object exists, a duration that the painting exists ... my most didactic works."

Indeed, humans need new ways of perceiving time. Plastic is made from prehistoric fossils, a time too distant for the average person to understand. As far as we know, it may never decompose, and yet every day we casually fling chunks of it into landfills.

We can't conceptualize this lifespan. It's an abstract number, an intellectual concept, and we cannot see it. It is this limit of human imagination that can harm us.

When Mick Jagger sings, "time is on my side," he taunts his listeners in the voice of the devil, because time is not on the side of humans. We remain forever caught up in its drama.

Somehow, painting—this ancient and simple desire—can reveal time. It can alter our temporal reality. It can make us feel time in ways we could never logically understand. In a picture, we can feel what has always been.

Acknowledgments

The artist would like to thank Eli Bonerz; Adam Michaels, Shannon Harvey, and Zoe Kauder Nalebuff at Inventory Press for making the book; Helen Molesworth and Ross Simonini for engaging with the work so generously; Rachel Uffner, Lucy Liu, and the team at Uffner & Liu; Pamela Echeverría, Luz Massot, and everyone at LABOR; James Bae; and most of all, Maggie, Lenni, Janet, Janine, and Grace.

Roger White: The Pedestrian
is published by
Inventory Press
2305 Hyperion Ave
Los Angeles, CA 90027
inventorypress.com

Copyediting and proofreading
Eugenia Bell

Design
IN-FO.CO

Printed and bound in Singapore
by Pristone

ISBN: 978-1-941753-82-8
LCCN: 2025933265

Distributed by
ARTBOOK | D.A.P.
75 Broad St, Suite 630
New York, NY 10004
artbook.com

Photo credits
Don Ross: 13–77, 95
Ramiro Chaves: 79–81
Charles White: 86–87, 91
Heather Rasmussen: 82–85, 93
JSP Art Photography: 89